A CLOCKWORK ORANGE 2004

Also by Anthony Burgess

A CLOCKWORK ORANGE

2004

by

Anthony Burgess

ARROW BOOKS

Arrow Books Limited
20 Vauxhall Bridge Road, London SW1V 2SA

An imprint of Random Century Group

London Melbourne Sydney Auckland
Johannesburg and agencies throughout
the world

First published by Hutchinson 1987
First published in this revised edition by Arrow 1990

Typeset by Rowland Phototypesetting Ltd
Bury St Edmunds, Suffolk
Printed and bound by
The Guernsey Press Co Ltd, Guernsey, CI

ISBN 0 09 976920 4

A CLOCKWORK ORANGE 2004

This version of *A Clockwork Orange* was presented by the Royal Shakespeare Company in 1990. I am grateful to its director, Ron Daniels, for his invaluable help with the adaptation.   A.B.

ACT ONE

A winter night in a capital city, in the unforseeable future. The winking electric sign of the Korova Milk Bar, with the word MOLOKO, shows that this could be beyond the Iron Curtain, since the letters are Cyrillic. This, on the other hand, may be a signmaker's whimsy.

ALEX, GEORGE, PETE *and* DIM. *Others there too.*

Music alongside the narrative, percussive, strong.

ALEX: There was me, that is Alex, and my three droogs, that is Pete, Georgie and Dim, Dim being really dim, the four of us dressed in the height of fashion, and we sat in the Korova Milk Bar making up our rassoodocks what to do with the evening, a flip dark chill winter bastard, though dry.

The Korova Milk Bar was a milk-plus mesto, and you may, O my brothers, have forgotten what these mestos were like, things changing so skorry these days, newspapers not being read much neither.

Well, what they sold there was milk plus something else, so you could peet it with synthemesc or dremcom which would give you a horrorshow fifteen minutes admiring Bog and All his Angels and Saints in your left shoe with lights bursting all over your mozg.

Or you could peet the old moloko with knives in it, as we used to say, and this would sharpen you up and make you ready for a bit of dirty twenty to one, for the crasting, the dratsing, and the old in-out-in-out.

3 DROOGS: What's it going to be then, eh?

ALEX: Out out out out.

GEORGE: Where out?

ALEX: Oh, just to keep walking and viddy what turns up, O my little brothers.

The day was very different from the night. The day was for starry ones, the old. The night belonged to me and my droogs and all the rest of the nadsats.

(DIRECTOR's note: The Nadsat Song may or may not be used. It should be possible to move straight into the first event of the evening.)

The Nadsat Song
DROOGS:
What's it going to be then, eh?
What's it going to be then, eh?
Tolchocking, dratsing and kicks in the yarblockos,
Thumps on the gulliver, fists in the plott.
Gromky great shooms to the bratchified millicent,
Viddy the krovvy pour out of his rot.
Ptitsas and cheenas and starry babushkas
– A crack in the kishkas real horrorshow hot.
Give it them whether they want it or not.

What's it going to be then, eh?
Deng in our carmans so no need for crasting
And making the gollybird cough up its guts.
Tolchocks and twenty-to-one in an alleyway,
Rookers for fisting and britvas for cuts.
What's it going to be then, eh?

As one door closes another one shuts.
Govoreet horrorshow, but me no buts.

The street. The lights of the milk bar wink out. A schoolmaster-type comes round the corner from the public biblio. Books under his arm and an umbrella.

ALEX: A malenky jest to start the evening with! (*They approach. Very politely.*) Pardon me, brother.

TEACHER JACK (*Scared but trying not to show it, loudly.*): Yes? What is it?

ALEX: I see you have books under your arm, brother. It is indeed a rare pleasure these days to come across somebody that still reads, brother.

JACK: Is it? Oh, I see.

ALEX: Yes. It would interest me greatly, brother, if you would kindly allow me to see what books those are that you have under your arm. I like nothing better in this world than a good clean book, brother.

JACK: Clean. Clean, eh?

PETE *grabs the books and hands them round. As there are only three:* DIM *doesn't get one.*

ALEX: 'Elementary Crystallography'. Excellent, really first class. But what is this here? What is this filthy slovo? I blush to look at this word. You disappoint me, brother, you do really.

JACK: But, but, but.

GEORGE: Now here is what I would call real dirt. There's one slovo beginning with an f and another with a c. 'The Miracle of the Snowflake'.

DIM (*Looking over* PETE's *shoulder and going as usual too far*):   Oh it says here what he done to her and there's a picture and all. Why, you're nothing but a filthy-minded old skitebird.

ALEX: An old man your age, brother. (*They begin to tear the books,* DIM *and* PETE *doing a tug of war*.) You deserve to be taught a lesson, brother, that you do.

JACK: But those are not mine. They are the property of the municipality. This is sheer wantoness! Vandal work!

PETE: There you are. There's the mackerel of the cornflake for you, you dirty reader of filth and nastiness.

They rough the man up, stamping on his glasses and stripping him down to his vest and long underpants, which get covered in blood. DIM *laughs his head off, dancing around with umbrella.*

DIM: Ho ho ho.

ALEX: You naughty old veck, you.

JACK: Oh oh oh.

JACK *staggers off while they rifle through his clothes, scatter his money.*

ALEX: Let it go, O my brothers. Our pockets were full of deng, so there was no real need from the point of view of crasting any more pretty polly to tolchock some chelloveck in an alley and viddy him swim in his red red krovvy while we counted the takings and divided by four. But money, as they say, isn't everything. We hadn't done much, I know, but that was only like the start of the evening and I make no appy polly loggies to thee or thine for that.

A DRUNK *comes on, singing.*

DRUNK: And I will go back to my darling,
When you, my darling, are gone.

ALEX: Viddy that, O my brothers. That I like not. I could never stand to viddy a moodge all filthy and burping and drunk, whatever his age might be.

DIM *fists the* DRUNK *in the mouth.*

DRUNK: Go on, do me in, you bastard cowards, I don't want to live anyway, not in a stinking world like this one.

ALEX: Oh. And what's stinking about it?

DRUNK: It's stinking because it lets the young get on to the old like you done and there's no law nor order no more. It's no world for any old man any longer, and that means that I'm not one bit scared of you, my boys, because I'm too drunk to feel the pain if you hit me and if you kill me I'll be glad to be dead. (*They just grin.*) So your worst you may do, you filthy cowardly hooligans. Prrrrzzzrr. (*He sings again.*)

Oh dear, dear land I fought for thee
And brought thee peace and victory.

ALEX: So we cracked into him lovely, grinning all over our litsos. But he still went on singing. The knives in the old moloko were starting to prick and stabbing away nice and horrorshow now.

They come across fat BILLYBOY *and his droogs about to perform some ultra-violence on a very young* GIRL. *The malchicks watch each other, quiet.*

ALEX: Well, if it isn't fat stinking billygoat Billyboy in poison. How art thou, thou globby bottle of cheap stinking chip-oil? Come and get one in the yarbles, if you have any yarbles, you eunuch jelly, thou.

The knives and bicycle chains come out. The GIRL *makes her getaway, screaming. There is now a fight . . .* DIM *is the most vigorous but least stylish of the four droogs. Dancing about with his razor,* ALEX *slashes. Blood pours down either side of* BILLYBOY's *face, while* LEO, *his number one, blinded by* DIM's *chain, howls and crawls about like an animal. Police sirens are heard. The droogs scatter. They run off, stopping in an alley, panting fast, then slower, then normal. In the blue dancing light from tellies in the flat blocks.*

ALEX: Viddy yourself, O Dim. Your platties are a grahzny mess and red red krovvy on your litso. (*They straighten his cravat, wipe the blood off his face, soaking a handkerchief in spit.*) Bog, the things we do for old Dim.

DIM *looks up at the sky.*

DIM: What's on them, I wonder. What would be up there on things like that?

ALEX: Come, gloopy bastard as thou art. Think not on them. There'll be life like down here most likely, with some getting knifed and others doing the knifing. And now, with the nochy still molodoy, let us be on our way, O my brothers. What we are after now is the old surprise visit. What's good for smecks and lashings of the ultra-violent.

DIM: Ho ho ho.

They go off, giggling madly.

Home of F. ALEXANDER. *Front door, window. Sofa, table with typewriter, scattered paper. Pile of typewritten sheets: A clockwork orange. There is a knock at the door, nice and gentle. Then louder. A young* WOMAN *draws the bolt, inches door open, still on the chain. Her husband works on, typing away.*

WOMAN: Yes? Who is it?

ALEX (*off*):   Pardon, madam, most sorry to disturb you, but my friend and me were out for a walk and my friend has taken bad all of a sudden with a very troublesome turn, and he is out there on the road, dead out groaning. Would you have the goodness to let me use your telephone to telephone for an ambulance?

WOMAN: We haven't got a telephone. I'm sorry but we haven't. You'll have to go somewhere else.

F.A.:   What is it, dear?

ALEX (*off*):   Well, could you of your goodness please let him have a cup of water? It's like a faint, you see. It seems as though he's passed out in a sort of fainting fit.

WOMAN: Wait. (*She leaves the door on the chain.*)

The four burst into the room. They wear masks. ALEX *is Disraeli,* PETE *is Elvis Presley,* GEORGE *is Henry VIII and* DIM *the poet P. B. Shelley.*

DISRAELI/ALEX: A nice malenky cottage, I'll say that. And the name on the gate. A gloomy sort of name: Home.

F.A.:   What is this? Who are you? How dare you enter my house without permission!

DISRAELI/ALEX: Never fear. If fear thou has in thy heart, O brother, pray banish it forthwith.

The WOMAN *returns with a glass of water.* ELVIS *and* HENRY VIII *go out to find the kitchen.* DISRAELI *picks up the pile of typing from the table.*

DISRAELI/ALEX: What is this, then?

F.A.:   That's just what I want to know. What is this? What do you want? Get out at once, before I throw you out. (SHELLEY *roars with laughter.*)

DISRAELI/ALEX: A book. It's a book what you have written of. I have ever had the most bezoomny admiration for them as can write books, brother. And the name is Alexander. There's a cohen sidence. *A Clockwork Orange.* A fair gloopy title. Who ever heard of a clockwork orange? 'The attempt to impose upon man, a creature of growth and capable of sweetness, to ooze juicily at the last round the bearded lips of God, to attempt to impose, I say, laws and conditions appropriate to a mechanical creation – against this I raise my sword pen.'

DISRAELI *and* SHELLEY *laugh.* DISRAELI *begins to tear the pages of the book.* ELVIS *and* HENRY VIII *come in from the kitchen, munching away, still with their masks on. They laugh as* F. ALEXANDER *goes for* DISRAELI *and* SHELLEY *intercepts him.*

ELVIS/PETE & HENRY VIII/GEORGE (*with mouths full of chocolate cake and beer*):   Haw Haw Haw.

DISRAELI/ALEX: Drop that mounch. I gave no permission. Grab hold of this veck here so he can viddy all and not get away. All right. Dim. Now for the other veshch, Bog help us all.

SHELLEY *pulls the* WOMAN'S *arms behind her back,* F. ALEXANDER *howls in rage, held down by* ELVIS *and* HENRY VIII. DISRAELI *untrusses and plunges.*

ALEX (*suddenly unmasking*):   Then after me it was right old Dim should have his turn, then Pete and George had theirs. Then there was like quiet and we were full of like hate, so we smashed what was left to be smashed. The writer veck and his zheena were not really there, bloody and torn and making noises. But they'd live.

*The Korova Milk Bar. In a corner a small group, who had been
rehearsing in a TV studio nearby. Somewhere,* P. R. DELTOID.
An orbiting loner also there, burbling.

ALEX: Fagged and shagged and fashed and bashed we got
back to the Korova Milk Bar, all going yawwwww and
exhibiting to moon and star and lamplight our back fillings,
because we were still only growing malchicks and had
school in the daytime.

DIM *prances around, fingerclicking.* ALEX *cracks the loner one
but he just goes on burbling.*

ALEX: In the land. In orbit. Stoned into a balloon. Very nice
but very cowardly. You were not put on this earth just to get
in touch with God.

In the silence at the end of the song, one of the GIRLS *from the
TV group suddenly can be heard singing the theme from the
Fourth Movement of Beethoven's Ninth.* ALEX *is enchanted.*

THE GIRL: Joy thou glorious spark of heaven,
             Daughter of Elysium,
             Hearts on fire, aroused, enraptured,
             To thy sacred shrine we come.
             Custom's bond no more can sever
             Those by thy sure magic tied.
             All mankind are loving brothers
             Where thy sacred wings abide.

DIM *lets off one of his vulgarities: a lip trump followed by a dog
howl, followed by two fingers pronging twice in the air,
followed by a guffaw.*

ALEX: Bastard. Filthy drooling mannerless bastard.

He leans across GEORGE *and fists him in the mouth.*

DIM: What for did you do that for?

ALEX: For being a bastard with no manners and not the dook of an idea how to comport yourself publicwise, O my brother.

DIM: I don't like you should do what you done then. And I'm not your brother no more and wouldn't want to be.

GEORGE (*sharp*): If you don't like this and you wouldn't want that, then you know what to do, little brother.

DIM: All right, Georgie. Let's not be starting.

ALEX: That's clean up to Dim. Dim can't go on all his jeezny being as a little child.

DIM: What natural right does he have to think he can give the orders and tolchock me whenever he likes? Yarbles is what I say to him, and I'd chain his glazzies out soon as look.

ALEX: Watch that. Do watch that, O Dim, if to continue to be on live thou dost wish.

DIM: Yarbles, great bolshy yarblockos to you. What you done then you had no right. I'll meet you with a chain or nozh or britva any time, not having you aiming tolchocks at me reasonless.

ALEX: A nozh scrap any time you say.

PETE: Oh now, don't, both of you malchicks. Droogs, aren't we? Droogs shouldn't behave thiswise. We mustn't let ourselves down.

ALEX: Dim has got to learn his place. Right?

GEORGE: Wait. What's all this about place? You Alexander the bolshy, then? This is the first I ever heard about lewdies learning their place.

PETE: If the truth is known, Alex, you shouldn't have given

old Dim that uncalled-for tolchock. I'll say it with all respect, but if it had been me you'd given it to you'd have to answer. I say no more. (*He drinks his milk.*)

ALEX: There has to be a leader. Discipline there has to be. Right? Pete? Georgie? (*No reaction.*) I have been in charge long now. We are all droogs but somebody has to be in charge. Right? Rightright? (*They nod, warily.*)

DIM (*surprisingly*): Right, right. Doobidoob. A bit tired, maybe, everybody is. Best not say any more. Bedways is rightways now, so best we go homeways. Right?

GEORGE & PETE: Right, right.

ALEX (*wrongfooted*): You understand about that tolchock on the rot, Dim. It was the music, see. I get all bezoomny when any veck interferes with a ptitsa singing, as it might be. Like that then.

DIM: Best we go off homeways, get a bit of spatchka. A long night for growing malchicks. Right?

GEORGE & PETE: Right, right.

ALEX: Well, then – same time, same place tomorrow?

GEORGE: Oh yes, I think that can be arranged.

Two POLICEMEN *approach.*

POLICEMAN 1: You lot know anything about the happenings at the home of one F. Alexander this night?

ALEX: Why, what happened?

POLICEMAN 1: Two hospitalizations. Very brutal. Very unpleasant.

POLICEMAN 2: Where've you lot been this evening?

ALEX: I don't go much for this nasty tone, these nasty insinuations. A very suspicious nature all this betokeneth, my little brother.

POLICEMAN 2:   We're only asking. We've got a job to do like anyone else.

POLICEMAN 1:   But I warn you, Alex boy . . .

ALEX: How do you know my name, you vonny bully?

POLICEMAN 1:   Everyone knows little Alex and his so-called droogs. Quite a famous young boy our Alex has become. But I warn you, next time I'll make sure you're in it, right up to the shiyah.

ALEX: Bog blast you to hell, you sod.

DROOGS (*handing them lip music*):   Brrrrzzzzzrrr.

ALEX: Same time, same place.

DIM (*still wiping blood from his mouth*):   And it is hoped that won't be no more of them singing ptitsas in here. Ho ho ho.

They go.

ALEX: So off we went our several ways.

ALEX: Where I lived was with my papapa and my mum in the flats of Municipal Flatblock 18A, between Kingsley Avenue and Wilsonsway. The lift had been tolchocked real horrorshow this night so I had to walk the ten floors up. I cursed and panted climbing, being tired in plott if not so much in brain. I wanted music very bad this evening. I wanted like a big feast of it before getting my passport stamped at sleep's frontier and the stripy shest lifted to let me through.
    I went into my own little room. My den. Here was my bed, my stereo, pride of my jeezny, my discs in their cupboard, and little speakers all arranged round the room, on ceilings,

walls, floors. So, lying on my bed slooshing the music, oh my brothers, I was like netted, meshed in the orchestra.

Now. I pulled the lovely Ninth out of its sleeve, so that Ludwig van was now nagoy too and I set the needle hissing on to the last movement, which was all bliss.

There it was then. Oh bliss bliss and heaven. I lay all nagoy, glazzies closed, rot open in bliss, slooshying the sluice of lovely sounds. Oh it was gorgeousness and gorgeosity made flesh, O my brothers . . . It was wonder of wonders . . . As I slooshied, my glazzies tight shut to shut in the bliss that was better than any synthemesc God, I knew such lovely pictures . . .

There were vecks and ptitsas lying on the ground screaming for mercy in my ha ha power and I was smecking all over my rot and grinding my boot in their litsos . . . There were devotchkas ripped and creeching against walls . . . I plunging like a shlaga into them . . . and then, lying there with glazzies tight shut, rookers behind my gulliver . . . I broke . . . spattered . . . cried aaaaaaaaah . . . with the bliss of it . . . and dropped off to sleep . . . still with Joy Joy Joy crashing . . . and howling away.

He sleeps. The music then dies away. His MOTHER *is there.*

MOTHER: It's gone eight, son. You don't want to be late for school again.

ALEX (*stirring*): A bit of pain in my gulliver. Leave us be. I'll sleep it off, be right as dodgers for this after.

MOTHER: I'll put your breakfast in the oven then, son. I'm off now.

ALEX *sleeps again. A doorbell goes brrr brrr brrr.*

DELTOID (*off*): Come on, then. Get out of it. I know you're in bed.

ALEX: Right right right.

ALEX *puts on his silk dressing gown and woolly slippers. In a filthy raincoat and looking shagged, in shambles* P. R. DELTOID, *a post corrective adviser.*

DELTOID: Ah, little Alex. I met your mother, yes. She said something about a pain somewhere. Hence not at school, yes.

ALEX: A rather intolerable pain in the head, brother, sir.

DELTOID: Sick tomorrow morning too so the same, yes. But very fit and well in the night. Little Alex, yes? Sit sit sit.

ALEX: Mr Deltoid, sir. To what do I owe the extreme pleasure? Is anything wrong?

DELTOID: Wrong? Why should you think in terms of anything being wrong? Have you been doing anything you shouldn't, yes?

ALEX: Just a manner of speech, Mr Deltoid, sir. But I was surprised to see you in the Korova Milk Bar, a mesto of that like depravity.

DELTOID: Depravity, eh? To me it is very much like a harmless milk bar. But I hear that the white milk can be a wrapper for certain drugs, drencom, synthemesc and the like, yes?

ALEX: Terrible, sir. Drugs, sir, can sap all the strength and goodness out of a malchick. Them I touch not, oh verily not.

DELTOID: No, yes. Have to keep up our strength to indulge in crimes of the night, don't we. To destroy, yes? Break. Steal. Commit mayhem. Slash. Soon you will kill, yes?

ALEX: Never, sir. Never not. Life is like sacred, Mr Deltoid, sir.

DELTOID: You watch out, little Alex. Next time it's not going
to be the Corrective School. Next time, it's going to be the
great barry hole. All my work ruined. Remember that. Yes.
And I will not speak up for you, oh no. I will say that you are
villainy incarnate. I will say that you are Original Sin
prowling the town.

ALEX: I've been doing nothing I shouldn't, sir. The millicents
have nothing on me, brother, sir, I mean.

DELTOID: Just because the police have not picked you up
lately doesn't mean you've not been up to some nastiness.
There was an assorted amount of it last night, wasn't there?
Oh nobody is going to prove anything as usual. But I'm
warning you, little Alex, being a good friend to you as
always, the one man in this sore and sick community who
wants to save you from your horrible self.

ALEX: I appreciate all that, sir, very sincerely.

DELTOID (*sneering*):   Yes, you do, don't you? Just watch it,
that's all, and keep your handsome young proboscis out of
the dirt, yes. Do I make myself clear?

ALEX: As an unmuddied lake, sir. Clear as an azure sky of
deepest summer. You can rely on me, sir. (*He smiles nicely.*)

DELTOID (*in great suffering*):   What gets into you all? We've
been studying the problem for damn well near a century, yes,
but we get no further with our studies. You've got a good
home, good loving parents, you've got not too bad of a
brain.

> What gets into you all?
> Theological evil?
> The devil stalking the streets?
> The weevil in the flour of life?

I repeat:
What gets into you all?

ALEX: Let me explain to you, oh my brothers,
As for him and the others,
It's no good saying a word to them.
It's never occurred to them that
Energy's something built into a boy.
But neither the church nor the state
Has taught us how to create,
So we've got to use energy to destroy.
Destruction's our ode to joy.

DELTOID: What gets into you all?
Is it biological? Drivel!
It's unambivalent sin.
It's the devil grinning within.
God help us all.

DELTOID *goes*. ALEX *alone*.

ALEX: All right. I do bad. And if I get loveted, well, too bad
for me, O my little brothers, and you can't run a country
with every chelloveck comporting himself in the manner of
the night. But this biting of the toe nails over what is the
cause of badness is what turns me into a fine laughing
malchick. They don't go into what is the cause of goodness,
so why the other shop? If lewdies are good, that's because
they like it and I wouldn't ever interfere with their pleasures,
and so of the other shop. And I was patronising the other
shop.

More, badness is of the self, the one, the you or me on our
oddy knockies and that self is made by old Bog in his great
pride and radosty. But the not-self cannot have the bad, they
of the government and the judges and the schools cannot
allow the bad because they cannot allow the self. And is not

our modern history the story of brave malenky selves fighting these big machines?

I'm serious with you, brothers, over this. What I do I do
because I like to do.

ALEX *finishes dressing for the night, whistling Beethoven. His*
FATHER *is there, eating a piece of pie.*

ALEX: Hi hi hi, there. Ready now for evening work to earn
that little bit. Yum yum, mum. Any of that for me?

FATHER: Not that I mean to pry, son, but where exactly do
you go to work of evenings?

ALEX (*as* MUM *brings him a piece of pie*):   Oh, it's mostly odd
things. Here and there, as it might be. I never ask for money,
do I? Not for clothes or for pleasures? All right then, why
ask?

FATHER: Sorry, son. But I get worried, sometimes. You can
laugh if you like, but last night I had this dream with you in it
and I didn't like it one bit.

ALEX: Oh? (*interested*) Yes?

FATHER: I saw you lying on the street. You had been beaten
by other boys, like the boys you used to go around with
before you were sent to that last Corrective School.

ALEX: Oh? Never worry about thine only son and heir, O my
papapa. Fear not. He canst taketh care of himself, verily.

FATHER: And you were like helpless in your blood and you
couldn't fight back.

ALEX (*taking money out of his pockets*):   Here, dad, it's not
much. It's what I earned last night. But perhaps for the
odd peet of Scotchman in the snug somewhere for you and
mum.

FATHER: Thanks, son. But we don't go out so much now, the streets being what they are. Still, thanks. I'll bring her home a bottle of something tomorrow.

ALEX *goes out with loving smiles all round.*

The hallway of the municipal flatblock. GEORGE *and* PETE, *waiting.* DIM *with a stick of black greasepaint or aerosol tracing filthy words on the wall.*

DIM: Wuh huh huh.

ALEX *enters.*

GEORGE & PETE: Well, hello.

ALEX *taken by surprise.*

DIM: He are here. (*He does a clumsy bit of dancing.*) He have arrived. Hooray.

GEORGE: We got worried. There we were awaiting and peeting away at the old moloko, and you might have been like offended by some veshch or other, so round we come to your abode. That's right, Pete, right?

PETE: Oh yes, right.

ALEX (*careful*): Appy polly loggies. I had something of a pain in the gulliver so had to sleep. Still, here we all are, ready for what the old nochy offers, yes?

GEORGE: Sorry about the pain. Using the gulliver too much like, maybe. Giving orders and discipline and such, perhaps. Sure the pain is gone?

The three droogs grin.

ALEX: Wait. This sarcasm, if I may call it such, does not become you, O my little friends. What goes on behind my sleeping back, eh? Now then, Dim, what does that great big horsy gape of a grin portent?

GEORGE: All right, no more picking on Dim, brother. That's part of the new way.

ALEX: New way? Let me slooshy more.

PETE: No offence, Alex, but we want to have things more democratic like. Not like you saying what to do and what not all the time. But no offence.

GEORGE: Offence is neither here nor elsewhere. It's the matter of who has ideas. What ideas has he had? (*He keeps his very bold eyes on* ALEX.): It's all the small stuff, malenky veshches like tonight. We're growing up, brothers.

ALEX (*he doesn't move*):   More. Let me slooshy more.

GEORGE: If you must have it, have it, then. We itty around, shop crasting and the like, coming out with a pitiful rookerful of cutter each. And there's Will the English in the Muscleman Coffee mesto saying he can fence anything that any malchick cares to try to crast. The shiny stuff, the ice.

ALEX: So. Since when have you been consorting and comporting with Will the English?

GEORGE: Now and again. Like last Sabbath, for instance. I can live my own jeezny, droogie, right? Right. The big big big money is available is what Will the English says.

ALEX: And what will you do with the big big big money as you so highfalutin call it? If you need an auto you pluck it from the trees. If you need pretty polly you take it. Yes? Why this sudden shilarny for being the big bloated capitalist?

GEORGE: Ah, you think and govoreet sometimes like a little child. Alex the not so large.

DIM: Huh huh huh.

GEORGE: Tonight we pull a mansize crast.

ALEX (*with great care, smiling*):   Good. Real horrorshow. Iniciative comes to them as wait. I have taught you much. Now tell me what you have in mind, Georgieboy?

GEORGE (*crafty*):   Oh, the old moloko plus first, would you not say. Something to sharpen us up, boy, but you especially, we having the start on you.

ALEX: You have govoreeted my thoughts for me. I was about to suggest the dear old Korova. Good good good. Lead, little Georgie. (*But suddenly*): Right George, now. Let's thou and me have all this out now, shall us? (*He whips out his razor.*)

GEORGE: Uh? (*His knife is also out.*)

DIM: Oh no, not right, that isn't. (*He makes to uncoil his chain.*)

PETE: Leave them, it's right like that.

GEORGE *and* ALEX, *look for openings,* GEORGE *lurching.* ALEX *goes ak ak ak with his razor and* GEORGE *drops his knife, his hand dribbling blood.*

ALEX: Now. O Dim the dim. Now we should know.

DIM: Aaaaaaaaaaarh.

DIM *snakes out the chain from his waist.* ALEX *keeps low but is whished badly on the back. Then* ALEX *cuts* DIM's *wrist.* DIM *drops his chain and tries to drink in the blood from his wrist and yowl at the same time.*

ALEX: Right, my droogies, anybody else interessovated in a bit of fillying, eh? Yes, Pete?

PETE: I never said anything. I never govoreeted one slovo. Look, old Dim's bleeding to death.

ALEX: Never. One can die but once. Dim died before he was born. That red red krovvy will soon stop. (ALEX *wraps his own clean handkerchief around* DIM*'s wrist.*) So we proceed under the like leadership of your little droog Alex. Alex the bolshy. Alexander the large. Right, Dim? Right, Georgie? Right right oh Pete of my heart? Just like before and all forgotten, right?

GEORGE: Right right right.

ALEX: And what mansize crast dids't thou in thy mind have, Georgieboy?

GEORGE: Oh, not tonight. Not this nochy, please.

ALEX: You're a big strong chelloveck, like us all. We're not little children, are we, Georgieboy?

GEORGE: It was this house, see. The one with two lamps outside. The one with the gloopy name, like.

ALEX: What gloopy name?

GEORGE: The Mansion or the Manse or some such piece of gloop. Where this starry ptitsa lives with all these very starry valuable veshches.

ALEX: Such as?

GEORGE: Gold and silver and like jewels. It was Will the English who like said.

ALEX: I viddy. I viddy horrorshow. Out in Old Town. (*Generous.*) Very good, Georgie. A good thought and one to be followed. Let us itty at once.

As they are going, ALEX *stops.*

ALEX: And so I led my three droogs out to my doom.

The manse in Old Town. A room full of antiques, an OLD WOMAN *feeding milk to her cats. The bell rings. Then again, more urgently. Then the* OLD WOMAN *speaks into the intercom.*

OLD WOMAN: Go away. Go away or I'll set my cats on to you.

ALEX (*over the intercom*):   Help, madam, please. My friend has just had a funny turn on the street. Let me phone for the doctor, please.

OLD WOMAN: Go away. Go away or I shoot. (*Giggles over the intercom and shhhh.*)

ALEX: Oh, please help, madam. My friend's like dying.

OLD WOMAN: Go away. I know your dirty tricks, making me open the door and then buy things I don't want. Go away or I'll ring for the police.

ALEX: Very well, madam. If you won't help I must take my suffering friend elsewhere. All right, old friend, you will surely meet some good samaritan some place other. This old lady perhaps cannot be blamed for being suspicious with so many scoundrels and rogues of the night about. No, indeed not.

There is silence. The OLD LADY *flipflaps away from the door. The cats purr and miaow. Suddenly* ALEX *is there, at first unseen.*

ALEX: The window was, as I had expected, closed but I outed my britva and cracked the glass with the bony handle thereof and I was, like getting into the bath, in.
      All this waste, brothers, all these rooms and but one starry

ptitsa and her kishkas and koshkas living on cream and fish heads like royal queens and princes.

I would take fair rookerfuls of like polezny stuff and go waltzing to the front door, showering gold and silver on my waiting droogs. I would do all on my oddy knocky, show those fickle droogs of mine that I was worth the three of them and more. They must learn about leadership.

ALEX (*appearing*): Hi hi hi. At last we meet. Our brief govoreet over the intercom was not, shall we say, satisfactory, yes? Let us admit, not oh verily not, you stinking starry old sharp.

OLD WOMAN (*very fierce*): How did you get in? Keep your distance, you villainous young toad, or I shall be forced to strike you. (*She raises her walking stick.*)

ALEX *advances slowly, catching sight of a bust of Beethoven.*

ALEX: Ah – Ludwig van I love. Lovely lovely and all for me. With this I start. (*He slips on a saucer of milk.*) Whoops!

OLD WOMAN (*quickly cracks him with her stick*): Toad, don't you touch my things.

ALEX: Naughty, naughty, naughty.

The OLD WOMAN *keeps cracking.*

OLD WOMAN: Wretched little slummy bedbug, breaking into real people's houses. I'll thrash you, beat you, pull out your fingernails, you poisonous young beetle. Out of here. I've had too much of it. Blast you, boy, I'll die peaceful.

ALEX: Die in your own time, you filthy old soomka. All I desire is share and share alike. You and yours have built the grahzny world we live in. So now you pay. Yes yes, pay.

The OLD WOMAN *continues to hit out at him. Incensed,* ALEX *cracks her on the head with the bust of Beethoven. She goes down.* ALEX *kicks at her but she does not move. Police sirens can be heard in the distance.* ALEX *makes for the door and undoes the locks. His three droogs move in.*

ALEX: Away. The rozzes are coming.

DIM: You stay to meet them, huh huh huh. (*His chain whisshes around* ALEX's *eyes.* ALEX *howls.*) I don't like you should do what you done to me, old droogy. Not right the way you tolchocked me like the way you done, brat. Ah. The rozzes are on their way. Hear that lovely shoom? You stay to meet them, huh huh huh.

The police cars have arrived. The three droogs belt off, DIM *still going huh huh huh.* ALEX *howls in pain, caught in the headlights of many police cars.*

POLICEMAN 1 (*over the loudhailer*):   A real pleasure this is. Little Alex all to our own selves.

ALEX: I'm blind, Bog bust and bleed you, you grahzny bastards.

POLICEMAN 1 (*laughing over the loudhailer*):   Language language.

Three policemen appear through the headlights. One examines the OLD WOMAN, *the others pin* ALEX *down roughly.*

ALEX: Bog murder you, you vonny stinking bastards. Where are the others? My stinking traitorous droogs? It was all their idea, brothers. They like forced me to do it. I'm innocent, Bog butcher you.

The two policemen are laughing and punching ALEX.

POLICEMAN 1:   Well, little Alex, we all look forward to a pleasant evening together, don't we not?

ALEX: It's those others. Georgie and Dim and Pete. No droogs of mine, the bastards.

POLICEMAN 1: Well, you got the whole evening to tell the story of how they led poor little innocent Alex astray.

POLICEMAN 3: I think she's had it. Can't be sure, need the doctor. Phone from the car. (*He goes.*)

ALEX: It was all their fault. The bastards will be peeting away in the old Moloko now. Pick them up, blast you, you vonny sods.

The police laugh and punch some more.

ALEX: Hell and blast you all, if all you bastards are on the side of Good then I'm glad I belong to the other shop.

As they pull him towards the police cars, P. R. DELTOID *appears. They meet in the glare of headlamps and flashing blue lights.*

DELTOID: So it's happened, Alex boy, yes? Just as I thought it would. Dear dear dear, yes. Evening, Inspector. Evening, evening all. Well, this is the end of the line for me, yes. Dear dear, this boy does look messy, doesn't he? Love's young nightmare, like. Just look at the state of him.

POLICEMAN 1: Violence makes violence. He resisted his lawful arresters.

DELTOID: End of the line, yes. So now he gets out of my soft probationary gloves into the calloused paws of the law. I suppose I'll have to be in court tomorrow.

ALEX: It wasn't me brother, sir. Speak up for me, sir, for I'm not so bad. I was led on by the treachery of others, sir.

POLICEMAN 2: Sings like a linnet. Sings the roof off lovely, he does that.

DELTOID: I'll speak. I'll be there tomorrow, fear not.

POLICEMAN 1:   If you'd like to give him a bash in the chops, sir, don't mind us. We'll hold him down. He must be another great disappointment to you.

DELTOID *goes up to* ALEX *and spits in his face, then wipes his mouth with the back of his hand.* ALEX *wipes and wipes his face with his bloody handkerchief.*

ALEX: Thank you, sir. Thank you very much, sir, that was real horrorshow, thank you. Did my hurt glazzies a lot of like good, sir, like the spit of the bearded veck that they hung on the cross on the halt and the lame.

P. R. DELTOID *walks away into the police car headlights.*

ALEX *continues.*

ALEX: All right, you grahzny bratchnies as you are, you vonning sods. Tonight you can have it, you cally animals. A signed confession, right right right. I'm not going to crawl around on my brooko any more, you merzky gets. You can have it then. The ultra-violence and drasting and tolchocking and the old in-out-in-out. Horrorshow, horrorshow. You can have it all.

The police doctor has examined the OLD LADY. *Suddenly there's silence.*

POLICEMAN 1 (*quiet*):   It looks like you can add a new one, right, doc?

The doctor nods gravely. They look at ALEX.

ALEX: Well, what? Are you not satisfied with beating me near to death? Have you some new torture for me, you bratchnies?

POLICEMAN 2: It'll be your own torture. I hope to God it'll torture you to madness.

ALEX (*realizing*): Snuffed it, has she? Well, well, real horrorshow.

POLICEMAN 3: Horrorshow is right.

ALEX: That's it. I'd done the lot, now. And me still only fifteen.

Staja Number 84F. The prison chapel. The plennies howl and weep through the hymn. WARDERS *shout.*

THE HYMN:　Weak tea are we, new-brewed,
　　　　　But stirring make all strong.
　　　　　We eat no angel's food,
　　　　　Our time of trial is long.
　　　　　But may we all begin
　　　　　To curse the strength of sin
　　　　　And all the devil's brood
　　　　　And let thy goodness in. Amen.

WARDERS: Stop talking there, bastards. I'm watching you, 920573. One on the turnip coming up for you, filth. Just you wait, 7749222.

CHAPLAIN: Louder, damn you, sing up.

The hymn comes to an end.

CHAPLAIN: What's it going to be then, eh? Is it going to be in and out and in and out of penal institutions, though more in than out for most of you, or are you going to attend to the divine word and realise the punishments that await the unrepentant sinner in the next world as well as in this? A lot of blasted idiots you are, selling your birthright for a saucer of cold porridge. The thrill of theft, of violence, the urge to live easy — is it worth it when we have proof, undeniable proof, incontrovertible evidence that hell exists? I know. I know, my friends.

A plenny lets out a shoom of lip music. Chassos rush in, hitting out at another plenny who screams.

PLENNY: It wasn't me! It was him!

It makes no difference. The CHAPLAIN *continues.*

CHAPLAIN: I have been informed in visions that there is a place, darker than any prison, hotter than any flame of human fire, where souls of unrepentant sinners like yourselves — and don't leer at me, damn you, don't laugh — like yourselves, I say, scream in endless and intolerable agony, their noses choked with the stink of filth, their mouths crammed with burning ordure, their skin rotting and peeling, a fireball spinning in their screaming guts. Yes, yes, yes, I *know*. Remember. Now go. May the Holy Trinity keep you always and make you good, amen.

The music of the voluntary is Bach's Choral Prelude Wachet Auf. *The prisoners are marched off, as* ALEX *comes on, in prison dress. He carries a well-thumbed Bible. Several plennies give* ALEX *the up-your-piping with their fingers.*

ALEX: So here I was in Staja Number 84F, in the height of prison fashion, of a very filthy like cal colour, the number sewn just above the old ticker tocker and on the back as well, so that going or coming I was 6655321 and not your little droog Alex not no longer.

A sort of filthy von rose from the plennies, not like real unwashed, not grazzy, my brothers, but a like dusty, greasy, hopeless sort of von. And I was thinking that perhaps being in this grahzny hellhole for two years, I had this von too, having become a real plenny myself, in spite of the great tenderness of my summers.

The CHAPLAIN *comes up to* ALEX.

CHAPLAIN: Thank you as always, little 6655321. The music you chose was, as always, admirable. Taste is a great thing. It leads one to the beautiful, and beauty, with truth and goodness, is one of the attributes of God.

ALEX: Music is heaven, sir, I see that. Beyond this horrible world of evil. I do so want goodness too, and that's the truth.

CHAPLAIN: The truth is in that holy book you handle, little 6655321. I am overjoyed that you read it. There is a text I would in particular ask you to ponder on. (*He grabs the Bible from* ALEX.) I see you read the Old Testament more than the New. But it is in the New that the word of the Lord most scintillatingly shines.

ALEX: Too much govoreeting and preachifying, sir.

CHAPLAIN: What's that, boy?

ALEX: I love the preachifying, sir.

CHAPLAIN: You have made notes here. What does this say? 'Yahudies tolchocking each other and then wiping off the red red krovvy and peeting their Hebrew vino and spatting with their wives like handmaidens.' What is all the blasphemy about?

ALEX: That was already in it when I got it, sir. Terrible.

CHAPLAIN: 'I would like to be dressed in the heighth of like Roman fashion and tolchock the bearded nagoy veck all the way to his crucifiction.' Corruption, corruption. I must give you another copy. There are plenty around. And what news have you got for me today, little 6655321?

ALEX (*not true*):   Well, sir, it has come through on the water pipes knock knock knockiknockiknock knockiknock that a consignment of cocaine has arrived by irregular means and that a cell somewhere along tier 5 is to be the centre of distribution.

CHAPLAIN: Good good good. I shall pass that on to Himself.

ALEX: Sir, I have done my best, have I not? I've tried to be good, sir, haven't I?

CHAPLAIN: I think that on the whole, 6655321, you have shown a genuine desire to reform. You will, if you continue in this manner, earn your remission with no trouble at all.

ALEX: But sir, how about this new thing they're all talking about? How about this new like treatment that gets you out in no time at all and makes sure you never get back in again?

CHAPLAIN: Oh? Where did you hear this? Who's been telling you these things?

ALEX: These things get around. Two warders talk, as it might be, a bit of old newspaper gets blown in the wind. How about you putting me in for this thing, sir, if I may be so bold as to make the suggestion?

CHAPLAIN (*smokes for a moment*):   I take it you're referring to the Ludovico Technique?

ALEX: I don't know what it's called, sir. But it gets you out quickly and makes sure that you don't get in again.

CHAPLAIN: That is so. That is quite so, 6655321. Of course, it's only in the very experimental stage at the moment.

ALEX: But it's being used here, isn't it, sir? Those new like white buildings by the South wall.

CHAPLAIN: It's not been used yet. Not in this prison, 6655321. Himself, the Governor, that is, has grave doubts about it. I must confess I share those doubts. The question is whether such a technique can make a man good. Goodness comes from within, 6655321. Goodness is something chosen. When a man cannot choose he ceases to be a man.

A guard approaches. The CHAPLAIN *continues.*

CHAPLAIN: We'll have a little chat about this some other time. Now 6655321, think on the divine suffering. Meditate on that, my boy.

ALEX *is led to his cell.*

WARDER: Here we are, sonny, back to the old waterhole.

The Prelude ends and there is silence.

The cell. ZOPHAR, WALL, BIG JEW, JOJOHN, *the* DOCTOR *and* ALEX, *smoking in silence. Warders on guard.*

ZOPHAR (*to no one in particular and anyway no one under-stands*):   And at that time you couldn't get hold of a poggy, not if you was to hand over ten million archiballs, so what I do do, eh, I goes down to Turkey's and says I've got this sprog on that tomorrow, see, and what can he do?

The cell door opens and PEDOFIL *is brought in.*

PEDOFIL: Eh? This one's full up. It's four to a cell, that's regulations. There's six in this one. I know my bleeding rights.

WARDER: Make the best of it. Share a bunk or sleep on the bleeding floor.

PEDOFIL: It's a bloody imposition, that's what it is. I demand my sodding rights.

WARDER: Rights, is it? All prisons is the same and it's you criminal bastards as is responsible. It's discipline you want. Discipline. A right dirty criminal world you lot are trying to build.

The cell door shuts.

PEDOFIL (*of the other plennies*):   Criminal. There's not one proper sodding criminal among the lot of you. Done more porridge than any of you and I know what's what. Have to sleep on the floor when that kid there has a bunk to himself. I'm not having it. (*Nobody is impressed.*) I've killed ten rozzes with one crack of my rooker . . . The kid's the youngest. He sleeps on the floor, not me.

JOJOHN: Leave him alone, you grahzny bastard.

PEDOFIL *settles on the floor, whining. Lights out. The cell is bathed in red from a lamp on the landing. The prisoners sleep. Warders on guard. After a moment* PEDOFIL *clambers on to* ALEX'*s bunk and starts stroking him, mumbling dirty love words.* ALEX *wakes and shoves him off the bunk. The others wake.*

ALEX: Vonny perverted bastard. Go on. Get on my bunk if you wish it. I fancy it no longer, if stinking perverted prestoopnicks are going to leap on me when I'm in no position to defend myself, being asleep. Go on. You have made it filthy and cally with your horrible vonny plott lying on it already.

BIG JEW: Not having that we're not, brotherth. Don't give in to the thquirt.

PEDOFIL: Crash your dermott, yid.

DOCTOR (*intervening*):   Come on, gentlemen, we don't want any trouble, do we?

PEDOFIL: Oww, yew wahnt noo moor trouble, is that it, Archiballs?

JOJOHN: If we can't sleep let's have some education. Our

new friend here had better be taught a lesson on how to be a
better boy in future.

PEDOFIL: Kish and kosh and koosh, you little terror.

Then it starts, gently. PEDOFIL *makes little noises as he's held
against the bars and the prisoners hit him. He starts bleeding.*

ALEX: Leave him to me, go on, let me have him now,
brothers.

BIG JEW: Yeth yeth, boyth, that'th fair. Thlosh him then,
Alekth.

They stand round while ALEX *joyously cracks at* PEDOFIL *in the
red light. He fists him all over and* PEDOFIL *crashes to the floor.*
ALEX *gives him a final kick. The whole tier seems to be awake.
There is screaming and banging with tin mugs on cell bars.
Shouts of* 'Shut it' *and* 'Close that hole' *over the tannoy system.
Warders rush around banging the cell doors with their sticks.
Then suddenly, silence.* PEDOFIL *still lies on the floor.* ALEX
tries to move him with his bare feet.

DOCTOR: Very unfortunate. A heart attack, that's what it
must have been. You really shouldn't have gone for him like
that. It was most ill-advised, really.

ALEX: Me? Come on, doc, you weren't that backward yourself in giving him a sly bit of fist.

They all look at ALEX.

ALEX: What you all vidding me like that for?

BIG JEW: Alekth, you were too impetuouth. That latht kick
wath a very very nathty one.

ALEX: Who started it, eh? I only got in at the end, didn't I? It
was your idea, Jojohn.

DOCTOR: Nobody will deny having a little hit at the man, to teach him a salutary lesson so to speak, but it's apparent that you, my dear boy, with the forcefulness and, shall I say, needlessness of youth, dealt him the coo de grass. It's a great pity.

ALEX: Traitors. Traitors and liars. Just like before, when my so-called droogs left me helpless in my own blood. There's no trust anywhere in the world, Bog blast you.

The WARDER *enters, agitated.*

WARDER: Get lined up. It's the governor and some big bugger coming. Special inspection and not one word of warning. Jesus. Hey you, get up.

ALEX: He can't. He's like snuffed it. These bratchnies here tolchocked him real brutal and nasty.

DOCTOR: Dear dear dear, Alex. The truth and youth do not go well together, do they?

WARDER (*bawling*): 'Shun!

The order is obeyed, with JOJOHN *and* BIG JEW *thoughtfully lifting the corpse and holding him upright. The* GOVERNOR *and the* MINISTER OF INTERIOR *come in.*

GOVERNOR: What's the matter with that man?

DOCTOR (*suavely*): Asleep on his feet, sir. He has no bunk. A common complaint in this prison, if I may say so. Over-crowding is an endemic problem.

WARDER: You shut your hole when the governor speaks to you.

MINISTER: Well, that's the horse's mouth. The situation is appalling. Cram criminals together and you get concen-trated criminality, crime in the midst of punishment. Furthermore, common criminals are pre-empting the space we may soon require for political offenders.

GOVERNOR: Well, what can be done, sir?

MINISTER: You know the solution, Gibson. The Government cannot be concerned any longer with outmoded penological theories.

GOVERNOR: I have my doubts, minister. An eye for an eye, I say. If someone hits you, you hit back, do you not? Why should not the State, very severely hit by these brutal hooligans, also not hit back? But the new view is that we turn the bad into the good. All of which seems to me grossly unjust. Hm? Besides, this new technique is hardly sufficiently advanced to justify the use of this prison as a –

MINISTER: As a trail-blazer. But there are certain urgencies. Political urgencies, to be candid. And I have every confidence in Brodsky. Common criminals like this unsavoury crowd can best be dealt with on a purely curative basis. Kill the criminal reflex, no more than that. Full implementation in a year's time – that's the government's policy. Punishment means nothing to them. You can see that. They enjoy their so-called punishment. They start murdering each other.

JOJOHN *and* BIG JEW *exchange a look, shrug and then let the body fall.*

MINISTER: Exactly.

ALEX: With respect, sir, I object very strongly to what you govoreeted just then. I am not a common criminal, sir, and I am not like unsavoury. The others may be unsavoury, but I am not.

WARDER: You shut your bleeding hole, you. This is the Minister of the Inferior.

MINISTER: Interior. All right. You can start with him. He's young, bold, vicious. Brodsky will deal with him. This vicious young hoodlum will be transformed out of all recognition. He might as well start now. And this creature, of course, may be delivered to the morgue, if there's room. Come, Geoffrey. (*He goes.*)

(DIRECTOR's *note: Should it be required the* WARDERS *can sing a lullaby*):

WARDERS: Discipline, discipline,
          Let's have discipline,
          Give him a haircut and a shave.
          Courtesy, deference –
          That's with reference
          To the foul way you behave.
          The names you call us
          Quite appal us –
          We're going to knock you into shape.
          You're going to suffer,
          You duffed up duffer,
          You jabbering gibbering ape.

          Discipline, discipline,
          Real live discipline,
          Like what you get in a war.
          When we've got through with you,
          What can they do with you?
          Use you for swabbing the floor.
          You're going to college
          To get some knowledge
          Of how to behave and how.
          So here comes discipline,
          Discipline, discipline,
          Here comes discipline now.

The new white buildings. A nice white clean bedroom. ALEX *is brought in a beautiful set of green pyjamas.*

ORDERLY: Well, Alex boy, little 6655321 as was, you have copped it lucky and make no mistake. You are really going to enjoy it here.

WARDER: You watch this one, right? A right brutal bastard he has been. And will be again, in spite of him sucking up to the Prison Chaplain and reading the Bible.

ORDERLY: Oh, we don't anticipate any trouble. We're going to be friends, aren't we? (*He goes.*)

ALEX's *breakfast is brought to him.*

ALEX: Oh. Eggiwegs and lomticks of spick and kleb and butter and the old moloko. With no knives or synthemesc in it, eh? Hohoho. Real Horrorshow.

WARDER: It's nice to know somebody's happy.

The CHAPLAIN *enters, sits on the edge of the bed.* ALEX *scoffs his breakfast.*

CHAPLAIN: Oh, little 6655321. (*To the orderly*): Wait outside, eh? (*The orderly does.*) One thing I want you to understand, boy, is that this is nothing to do with me. Were it expedient I would protest about it, but it is not expedient. There is the question of the weakness of my own voice when set against the shout of certain more powerful elements in the polity. Do I make myself clear? (ALEX, *mouth full, nods.*) Very hard ethical questions are involved. You are to be made into a good boy, 6655321. Never again will you desire to commit acts of violence against the State.

ALEX: It will be nice to be good, sir.

CHAPLAIN: Oh, little 6655321. It may not be nice to be good.

It may be horrible to be good. I realise how self-contradictory that sounds. I know I shall have many sleepless nights about this. What does God want? Does God want goodness or the choice of goodness? Is the man who chooses the bad perhaps in some way better than a man who has the good imposed upon him? (*He drinks from a hip flask.*) Deep and hard questions, little 6655321. But all I want to say to you now is this: if ever you look back to these times and remember me, the lowest and humblest of all God's servitors, do not, I pray, think evil of me in your heart, thinking me in any way involved in what is happening to you. (*He drinks.* ALEX *lights the cigarette that had come with his breakfast.*) And now, talking of praying. I realise sadly that there is little point in praying for you. You are to pass now to a region beyond the reach of prayer. A terrible thing to consider. And yet in choosing to be deprived of the ability to make an ethical choice, you have in a sense really chosen the good. So I shall like to think. So God help us all, I shall like to think. (*He drinks and starts to cry.*) All may be well, who knows. God works in a mysterious way. (*He begins to sing a hymn as he makes his way out.*)

DR BRANOM (*a woman*) *comes in.*

BRANOM: My name is Dr Branom. I'm Dr Brodsky's assistant. With your permission, I'll just give you the usual brief examination. (*She takes the stetho out of her pocket and examines* ALEX.) You enjoyed your breakfast, Alex?

ALEX: Oh yes, doctor, miss. Real horrorshow. What exactly is it, miss, doctor, that you're going to do?

BRANOM: Oh, it's quite simple, really. We just show you some films. And we record your reactions to them.

ALEX: Films? You mean like the sinny?

BRANOM: They'll be special films. Very special films.

The orderly brings DR BRANOM *a hypodermic. She injects* ALEX's *arm*

BRANOM: Yes, you seem to be quite a fit young boy. A bit undernourished perhaps. That will be the fault of the prison food. So, after every meal we shall be giving you a shot in the arm. That should help.

ALEX: Vitamins, miss, doctor, will it be?

BRANOM: Something like that. Just a jab in the arm after every meal. Put your pyjama top back on. You'll be having your first session right away.

The orderly comes in with a wheelchair.

ALEX: What giveth then, brother? I can walk, surely, to wherever we have to itty to.

ORDERLY: Best I push you there.

As ALEX *gets out of bed, he feels a bit weak. He's wheeled away by the orderly.*

ORDERLY: In a fortnight or so
He's going to be free.

ALEX: Free as a bee.

ORDERLY: Or a fly or a flee.

ALEX: Free as the sea.

ORDERLY: Or a chestnut tree.

BOTH: Free free free.

ORDERLY: In a fortnight or so
He's going to be free

ALEX: I'll soon be free

ORDERLY: Free as you and me,
               If we're truly free.

ALEX: It's the thing that we
               Always want to be –

BOTH: Free free free.

ALEX: Whoopee!

The experiment room. Wall with holes for projectors, stereo speakers, bank of computers. A chair with wires running from it. Other white-coated attendants. Very quiet. Very white. Someone coughs kashl kashl kashl as ALEX, *very weak is helped out of his wheelchair. Behind frosted glass, shadows of people moving.*

ALEX (*limply*):   Morning all. (*As his head is strapped in*): What's this for?

BRANOM: To keep your head still and to make sure you look at the screen.

ALEX: But I want to look. I love the movies. (*Lid locks are fitted to his eyes.*) What's these things on my glazzies for then?

BRANOM: Once you close your eyes the machine fails to register.

ALEX: But I want to viddy. I've been brought here to viddy films and viddy films I shall.

BRANOM: You never know. Oh you never know. Trust us, Alex. It's better this way.

ALEX: This must be a real horrorshow film if you're so keen on my viddying it.

BRANOM: Horrorshow is right, Alex. A real show of horrors.

BRODSKY (*coming in smiling*):   Aha. There you are. My name is Dr Brodsky. Everything ready?

Whisperings of 'Right right right'.

ORDERLY: I'll leave you now. Hope you enjoy the show.

Lights go out. The projector flashes. Pictures could fill the white walls. Soundtrack from film hardly perceived, beatings, groans, screams, gunshots and, quieter, music.

BRODSKY: A typical street scene of our time. Vicious teenage hoodlums beating up an old woman. See the blood – it splashes the camera lens. Hear the crack of bones breaking. Now the scene changes. The girl on the pavement is only ten. Her assailants are four in number. The rape is brutal. At the end she becomes a thing disposable. Torn to pieces. A gunshot up her –

ALEX (*in pain*):   No no no.

BRODSKY: No? But this is the sort of thing you like, you and your generation.

BRANOM: Reaction eight point seven.

BRODSKY: Promising.

ALEX: I want to be sick. Please let me be sick. Please bring something for me to be sick into.

BRODSKY: Imagination, only. You've nothing to worry about. Next film coming up.

The music on the sound track seems louder. Terrible screams.

BRODSKY: A Japanese prison of war camp in World War Two. Torture. Soldiers are being fixed to trees with nails and are having fires lit under them. A sharp knife disembowels a prisoner live. Now see – a decapitation. Head off as clean as a whistle – see. Headless though he is, the dead man runs around for a short while in total nervous automatism, blood like a fountain out of his neck. The torturers laugh.

ALEX: Stop it. Stop the film.

BRODSKY: Stop it? We've only just started.

ALEX: It's not fair. It's a sin.

BRANOM: First class. You're doing really well. Ten point four five.

ALEX: You disgusting sods. It's a sin, that's what it is, a filthy unforgivable sin, you bratchnies.

BRODSKY: What's all this about sin, eh?

ALEX: That. Using Ludwig van like that. He did no harm to anyone. Beethoven just wrote music. (*He retches.*) He gave heaven and you turn it into hell.

BRODSKY: I don't think I quite understand.

BRANOM: That is Beethoven on the sound track. The Scherzo of the Ninth Symphony.

ALEX: Give me a drink, for Bog's sake.

BRODSKY: Lights. Fetch him a carafe of ice-cold water. (*This is done.*) Loosen him. So you're keen on music. I know nothing of it myself. I just find it a convenient heightener of emotion, a discardable luxury, like marihuana and cheap sweets. Well, well. Now tell me what you think we're doing to you?

ALEX: You're making me feel ill. I'm ill when I look at that filthy pervert film of yours. But it's not really the film that's doing it. I feel that if you stop these films I'll stop feeling ill.

BRODSKY: Right. It's association, the oldest educational method in the world. And what really causes you to feel ill.

ALEX: These grahzny sodding veshches that come out of my gulliver and my plott, that's what it is.

BRODSKY: Quaint. The dialect of the tribe. Do you know anything of its provenance, Branom?

BRANOM: Russian and English getting together to make an international teenage patois. It's called Nadsat. Nadsat is the Russian suffix for teen. The two major political languages of the world reduced to an unpolitical jargon.

BRODSKY: Yes yes yes. Now then, violence is nauseating and you're – well, nauseated. Well, it isn't the wires. Those are for measuring your reactions. No. Flowing in your veins is a chemical substance – patented by the late Dr Ludovico.

ALEX: So it wasn't like vitamins?

BRODSKY: No, it wasn't like vitamins.

ALEX: Oh I viddy all now. A filthy cally vonny trick. An act of treachery, sod you, and you won't do it again.

BRODSKY: Don't fight against it, please. There's no point in your fighting. You can't get the better of us.

ALEX: Grazhny bratchnies. (*Snivelling*) I don't mind about the ultra-violence and all that cal. I put up with that. But it's not fair on the music. It's not fair I should feel ill when I'm slooshying lovely Ludwig van or G F Handel. All that shows you're an evil lot of bastards and I shall never forgive you, sods.

BRODSKY: What do you think of that, eh, Branom?

BRANOM: It seems we've given him a new disease. From now on music will make him vomit. Did you foresee this?

BRODSKY: No, but does it matter? Delimitation is always difficult. It's the quelling of the violent impulse that matters. We will cure him.

ALEX (*cunning*):   You needn't take it any further, sir. You've proved to me that all this dratsing and ultra-violence and killing is wrong. I've learned my lesson, sirs. I see now what I've never seen before. I'm cured, praise God.

BRODSKY: You're not cured yet. Only when your body reacts promptly and violently to violence, as to a snake, without further help from us, without medication, only then –

ALEX: But sir, miss, I see that it's wrong. It's wrong because it's against society, it's wrong because every veck on earth has the right to live and be happy without being beaten and tolchocked and knifed. I've learned a lot, really I have.

BRODSKY (*laughs*):   The heresy of an age of reason. I see what is right and I approve, but I do what is wrong. No, no, my boy, you must leave it all to us. But be cheerful about it. It will soon be over. In a fortnight you will be a free man. Lights. (*The lights dim once more.*) Now. Here we see some very recent film – a riot in London's East End, with the police as much responsible for the enormities enacted as the black, brown and white disaffected. Corpses in the gutter, corpses hanging from lamp posts, the torn and the eviscerated dying. This is the modern world. Sick, sick, mortally sick. 'How like a god' said Hamlet of humankind. Better to say 'How like a dog'. A dog, as Pavlov showed, can at least be conditioned by the control of its reflexes into behaving like a harmless machine. If mankind is to be saved, science must take over.

Science must dig its way into the human brain, crushing the instinct of aggression . . .

He is drowned by the glorious Ninth. ALEX *in despair. End of Act One.*

ACT TWO

Alex's room in the new white buildings. ALEX *in a nightmare: sounds of his dreams like the sound of the film clips, music very present. He suddenly wakes and is violently sick. He foots the door hard. He's crying.*

ALEX: Oh help help. I'm sick. I'm dying. Doctor. Doctor. Doctor, quick. Please.

ORDERLY: What is it? What goes on?

ALEX (*sobs boo hoo*):   Oh I'll die, I shall. Help. Boo hoo hoo.

ORDERLY: There there, wazzums all weepy then?

ALEX: I had a dream . . . like a nightmare. Nazi flags and streets that were all bomb holes . . . lewdies being shot against walls . . . this was real, very real . . . and Germans prodding like beseeching Jews . . . into mestos where they would all snuff it of poison gas . . . it was very real. It was horrible. (*He's ill again but manages to control himself.*)

BRANOM *has entered. The orderly goes for tea.*

BRANOM: Of course it was horrible. Violence is a very horrible thing. That's what you have learnt. Your body has learnt it.

ALEX: I don't understand about feeling ill like I did. I mean, doing it or watching it I used to feel real horrorshow. Now if I even dream —

BRANOM: The processes of life, the make-up of the human organism, who can fully understand these miracles? What is happening to you now is what should happen to any normal healthy human organism contemplating the actions of the forces of evil, the workings of the principle of destruction. You are being made healthy.

ALEX: What you've been doing is make me feel very ill.

BRANOM: Come, do you feel ill now? Drinking tea, resting, having a nice quiet chat with a friend?

ALEX: This Ludovico stuff must be there, cruising about in my krovvy. I will be sick always for ever and ever amen. Boo hoo hoo.

BRANOM (*shakes her head*):   You felt ill because you're getting better. When we're healthy we respond to the presence of the hateful with fear and nausea. You're becoming healthy, that's all. (*She smiles apologetically.*) In less than a fortnight you'll be a free man. Where will you go when you leave here?

ALEX: Oh, I shall go back to my pee and em.

BRANOM: Your —?

ALEX: My papapa and my mum in the dear old flatblock.

BRANOM: Oh. And have your parents been informed of your impending release?

ALEX (*relishing*):   No. It will be a nice surprise for them, that, won't it? Me just walking in through the door and saying: 'Here I am, a free man again.' Yes, real horrorshow.

BRANOM: So long as you have somewhere to live. And then there's the question of you getting a job, isn't there?

ALEX: Time enough for that. A nice malenky, holiday first. Or just lay back in my bed in my own little den and think over what to do now with my jeezny – with my life, that is.

BRANOM: We'll get you a list of jobs you can try for, anyway.

ALEX: Right right right.

BRANOM: We'll talk about it again?

ALEX: Right. Right right.

Laughing, DR BRANOM *leaves.*

ALEX: Less than a fortnight. O my brothers and friends, it was like an age. It was like the beginning of the world to the end of it. Every day this nurse ptitsa jabbed my rooker with a syringe and squirted this stuff in real brutal and I was wheeled off to this hell sinny and each day the sickness and gulliver pains and aches in the zoobies and horrible horrible thirst and I thought I have suffered to the heights and cannot suffer more.

The ORDERLY *is there with a laundry box.*

ORDERLY: Tomorrow, little friend, out out out. But you still have one big day in front of you. It's to be your passing-out day. (*Smiling.*) Today, little friend, we are letting you walk.

ALEX: Walk?

ORDERLY: Yes, yes, look not so astonished. You are to walk, me with you, of course. You are no longer to be carried in a wheelchair.

ALEX: How about my horrible morning injection? Don't I get that horrible sicky stuff rammed into my poor suffering rooker any more?

ORDERLY (*smiles*):   All over. For ever and ever amen. You've been permanently inoculated. You're on your own now, boy. Walking and all to the chamber of horrors. And look. (*He brings* ALEX's *nochy gear out of the laundry box.*)

ALEX: My platties of the night! All lovely and washed and ironed! My horrorshow kickboots! All polished! And my cut-throat britva, even, that I used in those old happy days! (*He frowns, puzzled.*) Wh –?

ORDERLY (*laughs*):   Come on then, my little tiger.

The experiment room, now changed: chairs arranged to house an audience. In come the MINISTER OF THE INTERIOR, *the* GOVERNOR, *the* WARDERS *of the Staja, the* CHAPLAIN, DRS BRODSKY *and* BRANOM. *Others.*

MINISTER: Take your seats, please. No noise. Try not to cough. Dr Brodsky, if you be so kind.

During BRODSKY's *speech,* ALEX *walks in uncertainly, in the glare of a followspot. He wears his old platties of the night.*

BRODSKY (*on mike*):   Aha. Now, ladies and gentlemen, we introduce the subject himself. Tomorrow we send him with confidence out into the world again, as decent a lad as you would meet on a May morning, inclined to the kindly word and the helpful act. What a change is here from the wretched hoodlum the State committed to unprofitable punishment some two years ago, unchanged after two years. Unchanged, do I say? Not quite. Prison taught him the false smile, the rubbed hands of hypocrisy, the fawning greased obsequious leer. Other vices it taught him too, as well as confirming him in those he had long practised before. But, ladies and gentlemen, enough of words. Actions speak louder than. Action now. Observe, all.

In the silence, a few titters. In another followspot, a big man,

strips of hair over his near-bald head. BALDY *goes up to* ALEX.
Followspots follow.

BALDY: Hello, heap of dirt. Pooh, you don't wash much, do
  you, judging from the horrible pong.

He stamps on ALEX's *feet, flicks his nose painfully, twists his
ear, bringing tears to his eyes. In the audience, more titters; a
couple of hawhawhaws.*

ALEX: What do you do that to me for? I've never done like
  wrong to you, brother.

BALDY: I do this (*does it*) and that (*that too*) and the other
  (*and that*) because I don't care for your horrible type. And if
  you want to do something about it, start start, please do.
  Come on and hit me. I want you to, yes, really. A real good
  crack across the jaw. Oh, I'm dying for it, really I am.

ALEX, *angered, makes to attack back, but is immediately
overwhelmed by sickness and pain. Sees he has to change the
way he feels about* BALDY, *reaches in his pockets for cigarettes.
He's crying.*

ALEX: I'd like to give you a cancer – a cigarette, brother, but I
  don't seem to have any.

BALDY: Wah wah. Boohoohoo. Cry, baby.

BALDY *flicks* ALEX's *nose again. Loud mirth from the audience.*
ALEX, *desperate.*

ALEX: Please let me do something for you, please. (*He brings
  his razor out.*) Please take this, please. A little present. Please
  have it.

BALDY: Keep your stinking bribes to yourself. You can't get
  around me that way. (*He knocks* ALEX's *razor to the floor.*)

Scum. Filth. Young dirt. (*He continues to dance round* ALEX *like a boxer, hitting, kicking.*)

ALEX: Please, brother, I must do something. Shall I clean your boots? Look, I'll get down and lick them.

ALEX *crouches and starts to lick* BALDY's *boots.* BALDY *kicks out.* ALEX *instinctively avoids the kick by grabbing* BALDY's *legs. This brings him hurtling down crack. There is loud laughter from the audience.* ALEX, *desperate to vomit, gives his hand to help up the startled* BALDY. *Angry,* BALDY *is about to punch* ALEX *hard.*

BRODSKY: Thank you, that will do very well.

Lights come up. BALDY *bows professionally implicating* ALEX *in the act with a generous gesture.*

BALDY: Well, everything's a lesson, isn't it, little friend? Learning all the time. (*He dances off.*)

BRODSKY: Our subject is, you see, impelled towards the good by, paradoxically, being impelled toward evil. The intention to act violently is accompanied by strong feelings of physical distress. To counter these the subject has to switch to a diametrically opposed attitude. Any questions?

CHAPLAIN: Choice. He has no real choice, has he? Self-interest, fear of physical pain, drove him to that grotesque act of self-abasement. Its insincerity was clearly to be seen. He ceases to be a wrongdoer. He ceases also to be a creature capable of moral choice.

BRODSKY: These are subtleties. We are not concerned with motive, with the higher ethics. We are concerned only with cutting down crime –

MINISTER: And with relieving the ghastly congestion in our prisons.

GOVERNOR: Hear hear.

They all start talking at once. ALEX, *totally ignored, suddenly speaks out.*

ALEX: Me, me, me. How about *me*? Where do I come into all this? Am I like just some animal or dog? Am I just to be like a clockwork orange?

There is silence at this. Then:

SOMEONE: You have no cause to grumble, boy. You made your choice. Whatever now ensues is what you yourself have chosen.

CHAPLAIN: Oh, if only I could believe that. He's transformed into a mere machine, fuelled by fear, incapable of hate, choice, worship or even human love.

AUDIENCE (*severally, appalled*): Love? *Love?* LOVE? *LOVE?*

BRODSKY (*after a silence, smiling*): I am glad, ladies and gentlemen, this question of Love has been raised. Now we shall see in action a manner of Love that was thought to be dead with the middle ages.

Lights go down again. In the second followspot a most beautiful young GIRL *appears, near nude. A sharp intake of breath from all the men present.* ALEX's *response is complex. He is deeply aroused but instantly feels terribly ill. As she touches him and he smells her perfume, the pain is agonizing. He has to think of her in a new way.*

ALEX (*screaming*): O most beautiful and beauteous of devotchkas. I throw like my heart at your feet for you to like trample all over. If I had a rose I would give it to you. If it was all rainy and cally now on the ground you could have my platties to walk on so as not to cover your dainty nogas with filth and cal. (*He feels the pain going away slightly.*) Let me worship you and be like your helper and protector from the wicked like world. (*The pain is almost gone.*) Let me be like your true knight. (*He grovels before her.*)

Lights come up to applause. The GIRL *dances off.*

BRODSKY: He will be your true Christian. Ready to turn the other cheek. Ready to be crucified rather than to crucify, sick at the very heart at the thought of even killing a fly.

ALEX *responds to that suggestion by vomiting.* BRODSKY, *ignoring him, continues.*

BRODSKY: Reclamation. Joy before the Angels of God.

MINISTER: The point is that it works.

CHAPLAIN: Oh, it works all right, God help the lot of us.

Photographs are taken of ALEX, *flash flash flash.* MINISTER *congratulates* BRODSKY. BRANOM *apart. The* CHAPLAIN *drinks.*

ALEX'*s room in the flatblock. Pictures of boxers on the walls, his stereo gone.*

ALEX (*to us*):   What's it going to be then, eh? That's what I asked myself. There I was, in my platties of the night of two years back, in the grey light of the dawn, having been waked up very very early to be told to get off out, to itty off home. They did not want to viddy Your Humble Friend and Narrator never not no more, O my brothers.

What it was going to be now, was homeways and a nice surprise for dadada and mum, their only son and heir back in the family bosom. And so the autobus to Kingsley Avenue, the flats of Flatblock 18A being just near. My heart was going clopclopclop with the like excitement.

ALEX *with key in his hand.* JOE *wakes.*

JOE: Who are you? Where did you get hold of a key? Out before I push your face in.

ALEX: How about you answering a few, brother? What are you doing here?

ALEX's MOTHER *appears*.

ALEX: Mum!

MOTHER: Oh, no. You've broken out. Oh Joe, whatever shall we do? We shall have the police here, oh oh oh. You bad, wicked boy, disgracing us like this.

ALEX: They let me out, mum. It was in the papers. Didn't you see?

MOTHER: So. What are you going to do now?

ALEX: Come home, mum, first. I mean, that's where I live. Sort of. Who's this then?

MOTHER: This is Joe. The lodger. He's got your room. We didn't think we'd be having you home for another eight years or so. Oh dear dear dear.

ALEX (*truculently*): Well, he'd better get out and give it back to me, hadn't he? (*His truculence makes him feel ill.*)

JOE: You. I've heard all about you, boy. I know what you've done, breaking the hearts of your poor grieving parents. So you're back, eh? Back to make life a misery for them all over again, is that it? Over my dead corpse you will, because they've let me be more like a son to them than a lodger. (*He puts a protective arm around* MUM.)

ALEX: So. So that's it then. Well. I give you five minootas to clear all these cally veshches out of my room . . .

ALEX, *angry, starts to retch*.

JOE: You filthy young swine.

ALEX: Shut your dirty fat hole, you.

ALEX *retches even more. His* FATHER *arrives, with the newspaper.*

JOE: Look, dad, look what we've got here.

FATHER: It's you, son. Cured, are you? This is all a bit . . . Not that we're not very pleased to see you again and a free man, too.

ALEX: Well, this is my room. This is my home, too. There's no denying that. And what, my dear pee and em, do you like propose for your only begotten pain in the —?

JOE: Watch that language, boy.

FATHER: All this needs thinking about, son. We can't very well just kick Joe out, not just like that, can we? I mean we made like an arrangement, didn't we, Joe? I mean, son, that room going begging.

ALEX: I viddy all. You got used to a bit of peace and you got used to a bit of extra pretty polly. That's the way it goes. And your son's been nothing but a terrible nuisance. (*Suddenly he is crying.*)

FATHER: Well, you see, son, Joe's paid next month's rent already. I mean, we can't just say to Joe to get out, can we, Joe?

JOE: It's you two I've got to think of, who've been like a father and mother to me. Would it be right or fair to go off and leave you to the tender mercies of this young monster who has been like no real son at all? He's weeping now, but that's his craft and artfulness. Let him go off. Let him learn the error of his ways and that a bad boy like he's been doesn't deserve such a good mum and dad as what he's had.

ALEX: All right. I know how things are now. Nobody wants or loves me. I've suffered and suffered and suffered and everybody wants me to go on suffering. Real horrorshow.

JOE: You've made others suffer. It's only right that you should suffer proper. I've been told everything that you've done, sitting at night round the family table. Made me real sick a lot of it did.

ALEX: What have you done with my own veshches, you horrible bastard? My stereo, my speakers, my disc cupboard?

FATHER: That was all took away, son, by the police. This new regulation, see, about compensation for victims.

ALEX: But she died. That one died.

FATHER: It was the cats, son. The police sold your things, clothes and all, to help with the looking after of the cats. That's the law, son.

ALEX: I wish I was back in prison. Dear old Staja as it was. I'm ittying off now. You won't ever viddy me no more and thank you very much. Let it lie heavy on your conscience.

FATHER: Don't take it like that, son.

ALEX *goes.* MUM *cries, comforted by* JOE.

The public biblio. Many sad OLD MEN *reading, or pretending to. Some asleep behind newspapers. Wheelchairs. Walking frames.*

ALEX: Ittying down the street in an aimless sort of way, cold too, all I felt I wanted was to be away from all this. I was wanting to cry and feeling like death was the only answer. And that be the end of Your Humble and Suffering Narrator: no more trouble to anybody any more. I thought how sorry everybody was going to be, pee and em and that cally vonny Joe who was a like usurper and also Dr Brodsky and Dr Branom and that Inferior Interior Minister. (*He has taken his razor out of his little bag but as he brings it to his throat he feels violently ill.*) But I felt very sick as I thought of myself going swishhh at myself and all my own red red krovvy flowing.

OLD MAN 1:   What is it, son? What's the trouble?

ALEX: I want to snuff it. I thought I might find a book on the best way of snuffing it with no pain. I've had it. Life's become too much for me.

OLD MAN 2 (JACK):   Shhhh.

OLD MAN 1:   You're too young for that, son. Why, you've got everything in front of you.

ALEX (*bitter*):   Yes, like a pair of false teeth.

OLD MAN 2 (JACK):   Shhhh.

ALEX *and* OLD MAN 2 *look at each other. Something clocks for both.*

OLD MAN 2:   I never forget the shape of anything. By God, you young swine, I've got you now.

ALEX *tries to get away. The* OLD MAN 2 *is on his feet, screaming.*

OLD MAN 2:   We have him. The poisonous young swine who ruined the books on Crystallography, rare books, books not to be obtained ever again, anywhere. A prize specimen of the cowardly brutal young. Here in our midst. He and his friends beat me and kicked me and thumped me. They stripped me and laughed at my blood and my moans. They kicked me off home, dazed and naked. Now he's here. At our mercy.

ALEX: That was over two years ago. I've been punished since then. I've learned my lesson.

OLD MAN 3:   Punishment, eh? You lot should be exterminated. Like so many noisome pests. Punishment indeed.

ALEX: All right, all right. Everybody's entitled to his opinion. Forgive me, all. I must go now.

OLD MAN 2 (JACK):   Don't let him go. We'll teach him all about punishment, the murderous young pig. Get him.

The OLD MEN *come hobbling and wheezing to have a go at* ALEX. *They grab him with trembling hands and punch him feebly.*

OLD MEN: Kill him.
            Stamp on him.
            Murder him.
            Kick his teeth in.
            Poor old Jack!
            Near killed poor old Jack he did!
            The young swine.

The army of panting, maddened OLD MEN *pursues* ALEX *round the reading room. An* ATTENDANT *rushes over.*

ATTENDANT: What goes on here? Stop it at once. This is a reading room. (*Nobody takes any notice.*) Right, I shall call the police.

ALEX: Yes yes yes, do that! Protect me from these old madmen.

ALEX *lets himself be held by the panting old men, who punch him feebly. His eyes shut tight.*

OLD MEN: Young swine.
                 Young murderer.
                 Hooligan.
                 Thug.
                 Kill him.

ALEX *tries to get away, is tripped up and engulfed. The* OLD MEN *start kicking him. Police whistles go.*

POLICEMAN 1:   All right, all right. Stop it now.

POLICEMAN 2:   There there there.

The young helmetted POLICEMEN (GEORGE, DIM *and* BILLY-BOY) *with great glee swish away at the* OLD MEN *with small whips.*

POLICEMAN 1:   There, you naughty boys. That should teach you to stop rioting and breaking the State's Peace, you wicked villains, you.

They drive away the near dying old avengers, laughing with the fun of it, and escape out of the biblio.

The deserted street. One of the policemen, REX, *holds* ALEX. ALEX *looks at the other three.*

GEORGE: Well well well well well. If it isn't little Alex. Very long time no viddy. How goes?

ALEX: Oh no.

DIM: Surprise, eh? Huh huh huh.

ALEX: Dim. I don't believe it. That the new night platties? It's like a rozz uniform. George! Billyboy!

BILLYBOY: Is. Not like. Evidence of the old glazzies. Nothing up our sleeves. No magic, droog. A job for those who are of job age. Good pay.

ALEX: You're too young. Much too young. They don't make rozzes of young malchicks of your age.

DIM: Was young. That's what we was, young droogie. And here now we are.

ALEX: I still can't believe it . . .

DIM: Previous experience as a villain a recommendation, eh? Ex-villains to catch real villains. Things have changed a bit, old droogie.

GEORGE (*to* REX):   More good would be done, I think, Rex, if we doled out a bit of the old summary. Boys will be boys, as always was. No need to go through the old station routine. This one here has been up to his old tricks, as we can well remember, though you, of course, can't. He has been attacking the aged and defenceless and they have properly been retaliating. But we must have our say in the State's name.

ALEX: What is all this? It was them that went for me, brothers. You're not on their side and can't be. You can't be, Dim. It was a veck we fillied with once in the old days trying to get his own malenky bit of revenge after all this long time.

DIM: Long time is right. I don't remember those days too horrorshow. Don't call me Dim no more either, little droogie. Officer, call me. Constable, call me.

BILLYBOY: Enough is remembered, though. Naughty little malchicks handy with cut-throat britvas – these must be kept under.

GEORGE: This will do. All lonely and lovely. Streets must be kept clean in more ways than one.

They take their jackets off.

GEORGE: Just a malenky bit of summary.

ALEX: And old Pete? What happened to old Pete?

DIM: Pete, oh yes, Pete. I seem to remember like the name.

REX *takes their jackets, moves away, and stands smoking a cancer. They stand for a moment.*

ALEX: Come. I just don't get this at all. The old days are dead and gone days. For what I did in the past I have been punished. I have been cured.

DIM: That was read out to us. The Super read all that out to us. He said it was a very good way.

ALEX: Read to you? You still too dim to read for yourself, O my brother.

DIM (*regretfully*):   Ah, not to speak like that. Not no more, droogie.

He punches ALEX *on the nose.*

GEORGE: Go on, do something.

ALEX (*nose bleeding and feeling sick*):   I can't. You viddy I can't. There was never any like trust. I was always on my oddy knockie.

GEORGE: Everything works out. Funny the way it does. You were very very naughty, Alex boy, grassing loud and clear about your old droogs.

ALEX: That was two years back. I had to. A court of law. The pravda, the whole pravda and nichevo but the. Besides, it's all over now.

GEORGE: Not all over, little bratty. Long memories some has.

The law has a long long memory. And it's the arm of the law now that doles out just a malenky bit of summary.

They beat up ALEX. REX *just smokes, holding their jackets.*

GEORGE: About enough, droogie, I should think, shouldn't you?

BILLYBOY: Be viddying you some more sometime, Alex.

DIM: Haw haw haw.

They go off, waving.

ALEX: I lay there, fagged and shagged, and then the rain started, all icy. I cried for myself, boo hoo hoo.

Home of F. ALEXANDER, *very bare. Books all round, tumbled papers. A sofa.* F. ALEXANDER *at his typewriter, as he was two years ago. A knock on the door. Then another, louder.* F. ALEXANDER *goes to the door.*

F.A.:   Yes, what is it?

ALEX (*on intercom*):   Oh, please help. I've been beaten by the police and just left to die in the road. Oh please give me a drink of something and a sit by the fire, please, sir.

F.A.:   Come in, whoever you are. God help you, you poor victim, come in and let's have a look at you.

ALEX *staggers in.*

F.A.:   God God God. Sit down. Dear dear dear. Somebody *has* beaten you up!

ALEX: The police. The horrible ghastly police.

F.A.:   All the same. Police and criminals. Terrorists, freedom fighters. Hijackers and liberators. Violence is sewn into our fabric. All the same. Take off those poor torn clothes and put on this old dressing gown. And these slippers. F. Alexander is the name. Perhaps you have heard of it.

ALEX *takes off his torn clothes, wincing, and dons the dressing gown.*

ALEX: Oh God! (*Very carefully*):   The name Alexander I know, sir. It is like my own eemya, sir.

F.A. (*alert*):   What? What's that? It is you! Wasn't that your picture in the papers this morning? (*He starts cleaning* ALEX's *wounds.*) It is you, poor victim. Tortured in prison and then thrown out to be tortured by the police. My heart goes out to you, you poor poor boy. Providence bade me pick you up in your blood.

ALEX (*eyes full of tears*):   How can I ever repay your kindness, sir.

F.A.:   There, there, there. You're a victim. A victim but also a weapon.

ALEX: Weapon? I don't quite pony that, sir.

F.A.:   You've sinned, I suppose. But your punishment has been out of all proportion. And I see that clearly – the marginal conditioning. Music and the sexual act. Literature and art, all a source now not of pleasure but of pain.

ALEX: That's right sir.

F.A.:   A man who cannot choose ceases to be a man.

ALEX: That's what the charles said, sir. The prison chaplain.

F.A.:   Did he? Did he? Of course he did. He'd have to, being a Christian. To turn a young man into a piece of clockwork should not surely be seen as any triumph for any government, save one that boasts of its repressiveness. They will do it to all of us. Since my poor wife left me I have given my life to fighting the evil that is abroad. And this government tries to stamp out evil with a worse evil. The book I wrote – itself a double victim. The manuscript torn up by wretched villains who then tore up my wife. The published book banned.

ALEX: What was the book called, sir?

F.A.: It is still called *A Clockwork Orange*. (*Is he mad?*) We all grow on the world tree in the world orchard that God planted and we are there because God has need of us to quench his thirsty love. Man is a fruit, a creature of juice and colour and perfume. They would tear out his pith and turn him into a robot. They will try to do it to us all. But you, poor victim, shall be a witness against them.

ALEX (*almost asleep*): Your wife, sir . . . has she gone and left you?

F.A.: Yes, left me. She died, you see. She was brutally ravished and beaten. The shock was very great. It was in this house. This room. I have had to steel myself to continue to live here, but she would have wished me to stay where her fragrant memory still lingers.

ALEX *is asleep*.

F.A.: Yes, yes, yes. You sleep now. Poor poor boy. You must have had a terrible time. A victim of the modern age, just as she was. Poor girl.

> She was all things to me,
> She was my body and my brain –
> Her hair was sheaves of autumn,
> Her smile was midsummer rain.
> She was all springs to me,
> The earth renewed every day.
> The leaves come green in April,
> Though they

Fall in the fall and burn.
She will not return.

Often in dreams I hear her
(I'm standing near her)
– She shakes her head.
'The futility of anger,
The sin of vengeance:
How can these profit the dead?'
But if they were here –
I'm living still –
My living will
Would seek to break, to rend, to kill –
Useless, useless, as she said.

She was all springs to me,
The earth renewed every day.
The leaves come green in April,
Though they
Fall in the fall and burn.
She will not return.

After a moment of stillness, F. ALEXANDER *leaves the room.*
ALEX *sleeps on.*

Late the following day. ALEX *still sleeps.* F. ALEXANDER *enters*
with breakfast. Draws back the curtains. Cold winter sunlight.
ALEX *wakes.*

F.A.:   You've slept long. I've been up hours, working.

ALEX: Writing another book, sir?

F.A.:   No no, not that, now. (*He cracks open an egg.*) No. I've
been on the phone to various people.

ALEX (*off guard*):   I thought you didn't have a phone.

F.A. (*alert*): Why? Why shouldn't you think I have a phone?

ALEX: Nothing, nothing, nothing.

F. ALEXANDER *looks at him closely, then goes on cheerfully eating his egg.*

F.A.: Yes, I've rung various people who will be interested in your case. The Government's big boast, you see, is the way it has dealt with crime these last months . . . proposing will-sapping techniques of conditioning . . . Before we know where we are, we shall have the full apparatus of totalitarianism.

ALEX: Dear dear dear. Where do I come into all this, sir?

F.A.: You are a living witness to these diabolical proposals. The people, the common people must know, must see. Will not the Government itself now decide what is and is not a crime and pump out the life and guts and will of whoever sees fit to displease the Government? I've written an article this morning, while you were sleeping. You shall sign it, poor boy, a record of what they've done to you.

ALEX: And what do you get out of all this, sir? I mean, besides the pretty polly you'll get for the article, as you call it? Why are you so hot and strong against this Government, if I may be so bold as to ask?

F.A. (*gritting his teeth*): Some of us have to fight. There are great traditions of Liberty to defend. I am no partisan man. Where I see the infamy I seek to erase it. Party names mean nothing. The tradition of Liberty means all. The common people will let it go, oh yes. They will sell liberty for a quieter life. That is why they must be prodded, prodded . . . (*He's picked up a fork and sticks it two or three times in the table, bending it. Is he completely mad? Then, kindly.*) Eat well, poor boy, poor victim of the modern world. Eat. Eat. Eat my egg as well.

ALEX: And what do I get out of this? What, sir, happens to me?

F.A.:   Eh? Oh, as I say, you're a living witness, poor boy.

The doorbell rings tingaling.

F.A.:   Ah, it will be these people. I'll go.

He lets in Z. DOLIN *and* D. B. DA SILVA.

DA SILVA: Hallo.

DOLIN (*coughing, cigarette in his mouth*):   Kashl kashl kashl. Filthy weather.

They come and stand, looking at ALEX *for a moment.*

DA SILVA: Good God.

DOLIN: Ahhhhhh. So for once we have teeth. God – his presence sets my brain whirring like clockwork.

DA SILVA: All right, all right, eh? What a superb device he can be, this boy.

DOLIN: If anything, of course, he could for preference look even iller and more zombyish than he does.

DA SILVA: Anything for the cause. No doubt we can think of something.

ALEX: What goes on, bratties? What dost thou in mind for thy little droog have?

F.A.:   Eh? Eh? That manner of voice pricks me. I heard it before. Once before.

ALEX: Oh that – it's what we call nadsat talk. All the teens use that, sir.

F.A. (*brooding*):   Strange. Strange. We've come into contact before, I'm sure we have.

DOLIN: Public meetings. We must exhibit him at public meetings.

DA SILVA: A ruined life is the approach. We must inflame all hearts. Kashl kashl kashl.

ALEX: And what is in this for me, brothers? Do I get to slooshy lovely Ludwig van without being sick? (*He feels sick!*) Ooh.

DA SILVA: Interesting. Interesting. I read that interview with the defecting Dr Branom. Not conditioning, she said – over-conditioning.

ALEX: There's only one veshch I require. To live a normal jeezny again. Can you do that?

DOLIN: Kashl kashl kashl. You will see, boy, that the Party will not be ungrateful. Oh no. There will be some very acceptable little surprise for you. Just you wait and see.

ALEX: Can you restore me to what I was? That's what I want to know.

DOLIN: Kashl kashl kashl. A martyr to the cause of liberty. You have your part to play in the overthrow of this damned Government and don't forget it. Meanwhile, we'll look after you.

Grinning, he strokes ALEX *as if he were a toy.*

ALEX: Stop it. I'm not a thing like to be used, brother. I'm not an idiot, you stupid bratchnies. Ordinary prestoopnicks are stupid, but I'm not ordinary and I'm not dim. Do you slooshy?

F.A.:   Dim. Dim. That was a name somewhere. Dim.

ALEX: Eh? What's Dim got to do with it? What do you know about Dim? Oh. Bog help us.

F.A.:   I could almost believe – but such things are impossible. For, by Christ, if he were, I'd tear him. I'd split him, by God, yes, yes, so I would –

DA SILVA: There there. It's all in the past. It was other people altogether. We must help this poor victim. He must help us. We must remember the future and our cause.

ALEX: I'll be ittying off.

DA SILVA: Ah no. We have you, friend, and we keep you. You stay here, boy. Everything will be all right, you'll see.

ALEX (*resistance making him sick*):   Whatever you say, brothers.

DOLIN: Good. Let's get started. (*To* F. ALEXANDER.) Come. Let's leave him here. You spend the night in my spare room. Tomorrow it begins. Truly. In earnest. Kashl Kashl Kashl.

They usher F. ALEXANDER *out.*

F.A.:   Dim dim dim. Who or what is dim?

DA SILVA: We are leaving you now. Work has to be done. Occupy yourself as best you can.

DOLIN (*returning*):   One thing. Kashl Kashl Kashl. You saw what stirred in the tortured memory of our friend F. Alexander. Was it, by chance – that is to say, did you . . . I think you know what I mean. We won't let it go any further.

ALEX: I've paid. Bog knows, I've paid for what I did. I've paid not only for like myself but for those bratchnicks too that called themselves my droogs. (*He feels violently sick again.*) I'll lay down a bit. I've been through terrible times.

DA SILVA (*smiling*):   You have. You do that. Rest, rest, per-
turbed spirit.

ALEX: Eh?

They are gone. There is silence. ALEX *appears to doze. The first
movement of Beethoven's Ninth can be heard quietly through
the walls of the room.* ALEX *wakes. For two seconds he listens
in interest and joy, but then it is the start of the pain and
sickness. He groans. He crawls off the sofa, going —*

ALEX: Oh oh oh. (*He bangs on the wall, screaming.*) Stop it,
Stop it. Turn it off.

*The music seems to get louder. He screams and screams but the
music only gets louder. He goes to the door, but it is locked
from the outside. He sticks his fingers in his ears but the music
is still louder. He cries.*

ALEX: Oh, what am I to do? Oh Bog in heaven, help me.

*He wanders through the room in despair; he tries to knock
himself senseless by banging his skull on the floor. The music is
louder still. Outside, a loudhailer cries 'Death to the government' and 'Death to tyranny'.*

ALEX: Death Death, one moment of pain and then sleep for
ever and ever and ever.

*In great agony he goes to the window and opens it. There's the
roar of traffic. He screams:*

ALEX: Goodbye. May God forgive you for a ruined jeezny.

*He leaps out of the window. He screams as he falls. The music
continues loud and then, suddenly, complete silence.*

*The hospital. Riot police confront an angry crowd. Petrol
bombs explode. There is a moment of stillness. Very cautiously*

DOLIN *and* DA SILVA *address the crowd through loudhailers.*

DA SILVA: The boy is a victim of the Criminal Reform Scheme.

DA SILVA & DOLIN: Out out out.

DOLIN: Murder is the Government's policy.

DA SILVA & DOLIN: Out out out.

DA SILVA: The people are on fire with indignation.

DA SILVA & DOLIN: Out out out.

DOLIN: This Government must go and go forever.

DA SILVA & DOLIN: Out out out.

The riot police advance in formation, chanting. DOLIN *and* DA SILVA *are arrested and beaten. The riot police retreat in formation.* DR BRANOM *and another* DOCTOR *arriving. Silence.*

BRANOM (*quietly*):   No physiological problems. Orthopaedically a success. What concerns us, of course, is the possibility that physical trauma may have undone Brodsky's conditioning.

OTHER DOCTOR: You want that to happen? After all your own work in the Pavlovian Institute?

BRANOM: The cause of this boy's near death has been well and accurately publicised. He tried to kill himself to escape from the music of Beethoven.

OTHER DOCTOR: I don't care much for Beethoven myself. Still, that was going too far. Sorry, Dr Branom. How soon can you tell?

BRANOM: Perhaps later today. I think he's already capable of submitting to a few tests.

OTHER DOCTOR: And the political angle?

BRANOM: What do you mean?

OTHER DOCTOR: Whatever you do you're caught up in the political angle. The Government wanted one thing. Now it's being forced to want another. Still the same Government. Same Minister of the Interior. Or Inferior.

BRANOM: There are some issues which are bigger than politics.

A NURSE *wheels on* ALEX, *bandaged, a drip into his arm. New voices chant* 'Out Out Out' *through loudhailers . . . The riot police exit in pursuit. More petrol bombs explode.*

BRANOM: Let him sleep. Tell me when he wakes up, nurse.

The CHAPLAIN *appears as in a dream.*

CHAPLAIN: Oh my son, my son. Religion is above politics, so I believed. But now I see how the two conjoin. It's all a matter of freedom of choice. We have the right to choose evil. Have we? Have we? Can I preach that from any pulpit? (*He drinks.*) But I would not stay, oh no. I could in no wise subscribe to what they are going to do to other prisoners, so I got out. Better if I go into retirement, my little beloved son in J.C.

He disappears. ALEX *wakes, as the chanting dies down.*

ALEX (*To the* NURSE *by his bed, who drops the book she has been reading*): What gives, O my little sister? Come thou and have a nice lay down with your malenky droog on this bed.

NURSE: Oh, you've recovered consciousness.

She goes for the doctor. ALEX'S FATHER *and* MOTHER *approach.*

ALEX: Well well well well well, what gives? What makes you think you are like welcome?

FATHER (*ashamed*):   You were in the papers, son. It said they had done great wrong to you. It said how the Government drove you to try and do yourself in. And it was our fault too, in a way, son.

ALEX: And how beeth thy new son Joe? Well and healthy and prosperous, I trust and pray.

MOTHER: Oh, Alex Alex. Owww.

FATHER: A very awkward thing, son. He got into a bit of trouble and was done by the police. They hit him about cruel.

ALEX: Really? Really? Such a good sort of chelloveck and all. Amazed proper I am. And where is the poor boy now?

MOTHER: Owwww. Gone back ooowwwwwwme.

ALEX: So now you're willing for me to move back in again and things be like they were before?

FATHER: Yes, son. Please, son.

ALEX: I'll consider it. I'll think about it real careful.

MOTHER: Owwwww.

ALEX: Ah, shut it or I'll give you something proper to yowl and creech about. Kick your zoobies in I will. (*That he does not feel sick at this, surprises him.*)

FATHER: That's no way to speak to your mother, son. After all, she brought you into the world.

ALEX: And a right grahzny vonny world too. (*His eyes shut tight.*) Go away now. I'll think about coming back.

MOTHER: Owwwww.

FATHER: Very good, son. Only get well.

They leave as the NURSE *returns, straightens sheets.*

ALEX: How long is it I've been in here?

NURSE: A week or so.

ALEX: What have they been doing to me?

NURSE: Well, you were all broken up and bruised and had sustained severe concussion and had lost a lot of blood. They've had to put all that right, haven't they?

ALEX: Has anyone been doing anything with my gulliver? I mean, have they been playing around with inside like my brain?

NURSE: Whatever they've done, it'll all be for the best.

BRANOM *comes in. She speaks gently.*

BRANOM: This won't take long. I'm going to show you some pictures. While you're looking at one, say exactly what comes into your mind. All right?

ALEX: Rightirightiright. What giveth? What new bezoomny idea does thou in mind have?

BRANOM: The first one. Yes?

ALEX: A bird nest, full of like eggs. Very very nice. Real horrorshow.

BRANOM: And what would you like to do about it?

ALEX: Oh. Smash them. Pick up the lot and like smash them against a wall or a cliff or something and then viddy them all smash up real horrorshow.

BRANOM: Good good.

She show him another picture.

ALEX: Bolshy great bird, like . . .

BRANOM: Peacock. You've seen them, haven't you? Look at
its lovely tail spread out in a beautiful fan.

ALEX: I would like –

BRANOM: Yes?

ALEX: To pull out like all those feathers in its tail and slooshy
it screech blue murder. For being so like boastful.

BRANOM: Good. Good good good. And this beautiful young
girl?

ALEX: Give her the old in-out-in-out real savage with lots of
ultra-violence.

BRANOM: And this scene of looting and killing in East
London?

ALEX: I'd like to put the boot straight in everybody's litso and
viddy the old red red krovvy spurting out.

BRANOM: Good. And this rather holy picture?

ALEX: The old nagoy droog of the prison charlie carrying his
cross up a hill. I'd like to hammer in the old nails bang bang.
Bang. Two for his rookers, one for the nogas. And one for
luck in the gulliver.

BRANOM: Good good good.

ALEX: What is all this?

BRANOM: Deep hypnopaedia. You seem to be cured.

ALEX: Cured? Me tied down to this bed and you say cured?
Kiss my sharries is what I govoreet in reply.

BRANOM: Wait. It won't be long now.

The riot police chant and protect the MINISTER *as he arrives with his* AIDE *and TV camera crew.*

ALEX: The Minister of the Inferior in poison. Well well well well well. What giveth then, old droogie?

AIDE: Speak more respectfully, boy, when addressing a minister of the Crown.

ALEX (*snarls*): Yarbles. Bolshy great yarblockos to thee and thine.

MINISTER: All right, all right. He speaks to me as a friend, don't you, son?

ALEX: I am everybody's friend. Except to my enemies.

MINISTER: And who are your enemies? Tell us that, my boy.

ALEX: All who do me wrong are my enemies.

MINISTER: Well, I and the Government of which I am a member want you to regard us as friends. Yes, friends. We have put you right, yes? Yes, Dr Branom?

BRANOM: Yes, Minister.

MINISTER: We never wished you harm, but there are some who did and do. And I think you know who those are. They wished to use you, yes, use you for base political ends. They would have been glad, yes, glad for you to be dead for those ends, then blame it all on the Government. I think you know who those men are. There is a man called F. Alexander, a writer of subversive literature, who has been howling for your blood. But you're safe from him now. We had him put away.

ALEX: He was supposed to be like a droog. Like a mother to me was what he was.

MINISTER: He was a menace. We put him away for his own protection. And also for yours.

ALEX: Kind. Most kind of thou.

MINISTER: When you leave here you will have no worries. We shall see to everything. A good job on a good salary. Because you are helping us.

ALEX: Am I?

MINISTER: We always help our friends, don't we?

He sits on the bed and puts his arm about ALEX. *The TV cameraman shouts* 'Smile'. ALEX *smiles without thinking. The TV camera rolls.*

MINISTER: Good boy. Good good boy. And now see, a present.

An expensive stereo is brought in by the AIDE.

AIDE: What shall it be? Mozart? Beethoven? Benjy Brit?

ALEX: The Ninth. The glorious Ninth.

And the ninth it is.

AIDE: Sign here, please.

ALEX *is offered a document. He signs. He closes his eyes, absorbed in the music.*

MINISTER: Good good boy.

The MINISTER, *his* AIDE *and camera crew leave.* ALEX *listens, his eyes shut.*

BRANOM: What do you see?

ALEX: I can viddy myself very clear running and running on like very light and mysterious nogas, carving the whole litso of the creeching world with my cut-throat britva. Oh, it is gorgeosity and yumyumyum.

BRANOM: You're cured all right.

ALEX: Yeah. Cured all right.

The Korova Milk Bar. LEN, RICK *and* BULLY, *in the height of fashion, with their droogie* ALEX, *who looks older than his new droogs. As before, other groups, gangs. Three* GIRLS *also in the height of fashion.* LONER *still there. They move to the strong rhythm of the music.*

ALEX: There was me, Your Humble Narrator, and my three droogs, that is Len, Rick and Bully, the four of us in the height of fashion, peeting the old moloko with knives in it, making up our rassoodocks what to do with the evening, a flip dark chill winter bastard though dry.

RICK: What's it going to be then?

BULLY (*of the three girls*): Hey, get in there we could, three of us. Old Len is not interested. Leave Len alone with his God.

ALEX: All right, Bully boy, thou cans't if thou wishest.

LEN: Yarbles yarbles. Where is the spirit of all for one and one for all, eh boy?

RICK: What's it going to be then, eh?

BULLY: Well, then, droogie, thou being the oldest and like the leader, what dost thou in mind for this kolonyiy winter nochy like have?

ALEX: Look, droogies. Tonight I am somehow just not in the like mood. You three go your own ways this nightwise, leaving me out out and out. Right?

RICK: What gives, bratty? What's coming over old Alex?

ALEX: Ah, to hell. I don't know. I don't know.

BULLY: Too tough a day, like, is that it? Rabbiting in the old Music Archives, gloopy sort of naz.

ALEX: Hey, a lot of nice free discs on the side and the pretty polly's horrorshow.

BULLY: Yeah? Pretty polly grows on trees, old droogie. It doesn't have to be earned, as well thou knowest. Took, that's all, just took, like.

ALEX: Ah, I've got some thinking to do.

All three make lip shooms at ALEX, *going* 'Haw haw haw'.

LONER (*burbling*):   Urchins of deadcast in the way-ho-hay.

He's tolchocked by BULLY.

ALEX: I'm getting just that bit tired, that I am. Babies, you lot. Scoffing and grinning and all you can do is smeck and give people bolshy cowardly tolchocks when they can't give them back.

BULLY: Well now, we always thought it was you was the king of that and also the teacher. Not well, that's the trouble with thou, old droogie.

ALEX: Listen. Tomorrow we shall meet same place same time, me hoping to be like a lot better. Right. Rightiright?

BULLY: Right. We can postpone till tomorrow what we had in mind. Namely, that bit of shop-crasting in Gagarin Street. Flip horrorshow takings there, droogs, for the having.

ALEX: No, you postpone nothing. You just carry on in your own like style. Now, itty off.

BULLY: Right. Right. If you won't itty with us, right sorry I am.

ALEX: You're not sorry, Bully boy. I viddy the old look in your glazzy – power, power and power. Well, take it. Heil, tovarish. Itty off and out. And the very best of.

The three droogs go, laughing, giving ALEX *the finger.*

DROOGS: What's it going to be then, eh? Out out out.

ALEX: Ah, to hell, to hell.

ALEX *sits by himself in the strange lights of the milk bar, all morose.*

ALEX: What was the matter with me these days I could not pony, O my brothers. It was like something soft getting into me – even the music I liked to slooshy was more like what they call Lieder, just a goloss and a piano, very quiet and like yearny . . . There was something happening inside me, and I wondered if it was like some disease or if it was what they had done to me that time, upsetting my gulliver and perhaps going to make me real bezoomny. What was it in me that was like changing? What was going to happen to me?

*A young couple (*PETE *and* GIRL*) come up to* ALEX. PETE *is looking a lot older, with an ordinary day suit and a hat on.*

PETE: It's little Alex, isn't it?

ALEX: Well well well, droogie, what gives? Very very long time no viddy, Pete – a long long long time since those dead and gone good days. And here is thou and here is I, and what news hast thou, old droogie?

GIRL (*giggly*):   He talks funny, doesn't he?

PETE (*to the girl*):   This is an old friend. His name is Alex. May I introduce my wife?

ALEX (*gaping*):   Wife? Wife wife wife? Ah, no, that cannot be. Too young art thou to be married, old droog. Impossible impossible.

GIRL (*giggling*):   Did you used to talk like that too?

PETE: Well, I'm nearly twenty. Old enough to be hitched and it's been two months already. You were very young and very forward, remember.

ALEX (*still gaping*):   Well. Over this get can I not, old droogie. Pete married. Well well well.

PETE: We have a small flat. I am earning very small money at State Marine Insurance, but things will get better, that I know. And Georgina here –

ALEX: What again is that name?

The GIRL *giggles.*

PETE: Georgina. Georgina works, too. Typing, you know. We manage, we manage. You must come and see us sometime. You still look very young despite all your terrible experiences. Yes yes yes, we've read all about them. But of course, you are very young still.

ALEX: Not so young. Eighteen. Just gone.

PETE: Eighteen, eh? As old as that. Well well well. Now we have to be going.

He looks lovingly at Georgina (the GIRL*) and she squeezes his hand.*

PETE: Yes, we're off to a little party at Greg's.

ALEX: Greg?

PETE: Oh, of course, you wouldn't know Greg, would you. Greg is after your time. He runs little parties, you know.

Mostly wine-cup and word-games. But very nice, very pleasant, you know. Harmless, if you see what I mean.

ALEX: Yes. Harmless Yes, yes, I viddy that real horrorshow.

The GIRL *giggles again.*

PETE: Come and see us, sometime.

They go off to their word games. ALEX *is still. There is a sense of desolation in his wonder.*

ALEX: Perhaps that was it! Perhaps I was not so young. Me. Not so young as I was. At my age, Wolfgang Amadeus had written concertos and symphonies and operas and all that cal – no, not cal, heavenly music. Felix M. too. And Benjy Britt. Not so young, then. But what was I going to do? Then, meeting Pete like that and Pete's wife, I viddied this vision. Your Humble Narrator Alex coming home from work and there was this ptitsa all welcoming and greeting like loving . . . and in a room a fire burning away and a good hot plate of dinner laid on the table . . . and I knew that in the room next to this room I should find what I really wanted . . . in a cot was laying gurgling goo goo goo my son . . . yes yes yes, brothers, my son. My son. And I felt this bolshy big hollow inside my plott. And I knew what was happening, O my brothers. Alex like groweth up, ah yes.

There it was. Youth must go, ah yes. But youth is only being in a way like it might be an animal. (*Somewhat helpless, perhaps.*) No, it's more like being one of those malenky toys you viddy being sold in the street, made out of tin with a spring inside and a handle, and you wind it up grr grr grr and off it itties in a straight line and bangs straight into things bang bang bang and doesn't pony what it's doing. That's being young. And the ultra-violence and the fillying and the crasting – that's being young too. And I look to the future and a son of my own who'll make the same like mistakes as I did just because he'll be young too. And I would explain all that to him, but then he would not understand or would not want to understand and would do all the veshches I had done and I would not be able to really stop him. And so it would itty on to like the end of the world.

But first of all, to find some devotchka or other who would be a mother to this son. Have to start on that tomorrow. A new like chapter beginning. That's what it's going to be as I come to the like end of this tale.

Tomorrow is all like sweet flowers and the vonny earth turning and turning and turning like a juicy orange in the gigantic rookers of old Bog himself. And there's the stars and the old Luna up there and your old droog Alex all on his oddy knocky, growing up. A terrible grahzny vonny world really, brothers and sisters.

And so farewell from your little droog. And to all others in this story profound shooms of lip music brrr. And they can kiss my sharries. But you, O my brothers, remember sometimes thy little Alex that was. Amen. And all that cal.

The full company has assembled.

CHORUS:
> Being young's a sort of sickness,
> Measles, mumps or chicken pox.
> Gather all your toys together
> Lock them in an iron box.
> That means tolchocks, crasting, dratsing,
> All of the things that suit a boy.
> When you build instead of busting,
> You can start your Ode to Joy.
>
> Do not be a clockwork orange,
> Freedom has a lovely voice.
> Here is good, and there is evil —

Look on both, then take your choice.
Sweet in juice and hue and aroma,
Let's not be changed to fruit machines.
Choice is free but seldom easy —
That's what human freedom means!